BROADCASTING
in a
Free Society

Lord Windlesham

Basil Blackwell · Oxford

© Lord Windlesham 1980

First published in 1980 by
Basil Blackwell Publisher
5 Alfred Street
Oxford OX1 4HB
England

British Library Cataloguing in Publication Data

Windlesham, Lord
    Broadcasting in a free society. – (Mainstream Series).
    1. Broadcasting – Great Britain – History
    2. Freedom of information – Great Britain –
    History – 20th century
    I. Title   II. Series
    323.44'5   HE8689.9.G7

ISBN 0-631-11371-1

Typeset by Cotswold Typesetting Ltd, Gloucester
Printed in Great Britain by
Billing and Sons Ltd,
Guildford, London, Oxford, Worcester

Contents

1

The Case for Press Freedom

I

A free press was described by Sir Winston Churchill towards the end of his life as one of the great democratic principles with a distinctively English character. As such he ranked it with Parliament, trial by jury and local government by local people.[1] It may be symptomatic of the decline which has taken place in national pride and confidence over the last twenty-five years that it is exactly these institutions, the most English part of our unwritten constitution, which are so often questioned today. There is, in fact, nothing particularly novel or remarkable about the state of conflict which exists between the press and those whose activities it reports and comments upon. On the contrary, as I shall argue, in any political society which is both vigorous and free, evidence of tension between the press and the politicians is inevitable and indeed healthy.

At times, particularly when the stakes are high, the habitual mistrust and suspicion with which politicians look on the press erupts into demands for repressive action. Churchill himself throughout his career was very sensitive to adverse comment in the press. On one occasion during the Second World War he even contemplated closing down under Defence Regulations his most persistent critic, the *Daily Mirror*, on the grounds that the newspaper had been publishing matter 'calculated to foment opposition to successful prosecution of the war'.[2] During the Suez crisis of 1956, Eden threatened action against the BBC[3] and went so far as to place a Foreign Office official in Bush House to vet BBC programmes for broadcasting overseas. As

Prime Minister Sir Harold Wilson always took a keen interest in the way in which the Labour Government was reported, and seldom hesitated to bring pressure to bear, particularly on the BBC.

Such pressures, however, remained no more than pressures; that is, strenuous attempts to influence and persuade. They fell a long way short of instructions that had to be obeyed without question. This immunity from government control lies at the heart of a free press. It is an indication of how deeply rooted the tradition had become, that from the early years of pre-war broadcasting in Britain freedom of the press came to include freedom of broadcasting, even though the institutional framework was quite different. Within the requirements of the law, broadcasters enjoyed the same freedom as print journalists to report and comment on the events, issues and controversies of the day. There were, it is true, certain restrictions imposed on the reporting of Parliament which to some extent continue to the present day. Parliament, for example, still excludes television cameras although the public, the press and more recently the radio microphone are all present. There are also a series of semi-formal agreements with the political parties over particular categories of broadcast programmes, while the requirements of editorial balance first set out in the Television Act, 1954 have been continued in subsequent legislation and regulation. The tradition of freedom from government control, however, and the sanction of public opinion on which it depends, is fundamentally the same. Freedom of the air stems directly from the principles of free speech and a free press.

It is curious that although so deeply embedded in the libertarian tradition, freedom of the press has never rated very high in the public mind. Although accepted in a general sort of way as being a useful constitutional right, especially as a check on the arbitrary use of power by government or other official bodies, few people bother to spend much time considering its implications. And yet the relationship of the press and broadcasting to government can say so much about the state of the society in which both function. It seems to be true of almost all forms of contemporary society, whether libertarian, authoritarian or Marxist, that the press will take on the coloration of the social and political structures within which it is contained.

Thus a scrutiny of the press and broadcasting as institutions, the controls to which they are subject, and the way in which they respond to political, social and economic pressures, can often reveal more about the distribution of power and the underlying assumptions about authority and freedom than reading what actually appears in the newspapers or is broadcast on television or radio.

If we start by considering the authoritarian approach towards the means of communication, it is immediately apparent that it is one with a long history. Communication is essentially a private act, the passing of a message from a sender to a receiver.[4] But when the spoken or written communication connects with a wider audience, or where the content of the message has a political overtone, from the earliest times the State took an interest. This process was greatly accelerated by the invention of printing in the fifteenth century. For the first time a mass public became possible, and before long the products of the printing press became the object of official interest and attention, soon leading to firm control. There was a respectable theory at hand to justify this control, and it was one that was reflected in the prevailing orthodoxy of the age.

In the thinking of the later Renaissance, as three American scholars named Siebert, Peterson and Schramm have explained in *Four Theories of the Press*:[5]

> ... truth was conceived to be, not the product of the great mass of people, but of a few wise men who were in a position to guide and direct their fellows. Thus truth was thought to be centred near the centre of power. The press therefore functioned from the top down. The rulers of the time used the press to inform the people of what the rulers thought they should know and the policies the rulers thought they should support. The Tudors and Stuarts maintained that the press belonged to the office of king and therefore was obligated to support the royal policy. Only by special permission was private ownership of the press permitted, and this permission could be withdrawn any time the obligation to support the royal policies was considered to have been dishonoured. Publishing was thus a sort of agreement between power source and publisher, in which

the former granted a monopoly right and the latter gave
support. But the power source kept the right to set and
change policy, the right to license, and in some cases the
right to censor.

II

The idea of the press as a privileged servant of the State is still
alive and flourishing in many parts of the world. Throughout
the Marxist world and in many of the authoritarian regimes of
the Third World, governments expect the press to support, if not
actively to promote and advance, the aims and policies of the
State. Too much attention given to matters that are considered
to be irrelevant or trivial is frowned upon, while an awareness
that in a different sort of society the press can at times preserve
the interests of its citizens by criticism of government has no
place at all in this concept. The duty of the mass media of
communication is firmly regarded as being to support the purposes of the State, and the purposes of the State are defined by
the government in power at the time.

Authoritarian policies determine practice over much of the
world today. In the Soviet Union and other Socialist states it
is quite open, explicit and unvarnished. Elsewhere, for example
in the developing countries of the Third World, affectionate
memories sometimes linger of the libertarian principles which
played such an important part in their grant of independence
from the colonial powers and are now incorporated in the
Charter of the United Nations and the Universal Declaration
of Human Rights. Thus attempts were made to graft on to the
constitution of the new state the familiar language of the Western
Democratic tradition. Only just below the surface, however,
lie profound and in present circumstances perhaps irreconcilable
differences.

The underlying issues were well illustrated at the Twentieth
General Conference of UNESCO which took place in Paris in
October and November 1978. Normally UNESCO conferences
attract little public attention and the Paris meeting would have
been no exception, but for one item on the agenda. This was
item 22, a draft declaration on the fundamental principles

governing the contribution of the mass media to strengthening peace and international understanding and to combating war propaganda, racialism and apartheid.[6]

The full text of the draft declaration, together with its preamble, ran to about 5000 words. It inspired more than 150 pages of amendments, including several rewritten versions of the original.[7] Even so, what appeared before the conference represented only the tip of a monumental iceberg of international debate, drafting and negotiation extending over several years. It is instructive to study this incident in a little detail since it provides insights into the way press freedom is looked upon in a context wider than our own. Since the early seventies UNESCO has interested itself in communications policy, partly no doubt in order to develop a new role for one of the conspicuously less successful international organizations, and partly to reflect and act as a focus for the growing demand from the Third World for a new world order in the field of communications as well as in economic development.

The idea of a new world information order, modelled on the concept of a new world economic order, has become part of the general currency of debate. There is little agreement, however, on what it would mean in practice. The most that can be said is that it stands for a series of arrangements different from those which prevail today. The embers of anti-colonialism are still smouldering, but more specifically one well-informed observer believes the often bitter criticism by Third World countries of the largely Western controlled media of international communication is rooted in three main arguments:

> The media are too powerful – they penetrate too widely and effectively. They represent an alien viewpoint, which they impress on nations trying to build an independent, modern identity. And they lack the attributes – of accuracy and objectivity, for example – on which they have based their claims to pre-eminence.[8]

The history of the draft declaration was as involved as it was lengthy. Its origins went back to a debate at the UNESCO General Conference in 1970. Questionnaires, meetings of experts, drafting and further debate continued over the next five years. By 1976 Third World opinion was hardening, as indicated by conferences held in Costa Rica and Colombo that year. At a meeting of Latin American governments convened by UNESCO in Costa Rica in July 1976 the principle of State involvement in national communications policies was endorsed, with a specific reference to the need to integrate mass communications media with national planning. This theme, the interdependence of information and economic development, was becoming established as an accepted canon of Third World ideology, and one that was encouraged by the Soviet Union and other Communist States. A month later, for instance, the Non-Aligned Summit meeting in Colombo called for a New Order for Information, proclaiming that the emancipation and development of national information media was an integral part of the overall struggle for political, economic and social independence.[9]

By November 1976, when a Russian-inspired draft declaration on the use of the mass media was put before the Nineteenth General Conference of UNESCO in Nairobi, the controversy reached a public climax and the subsequent divisions between the Western and Third World members split UNESCO deeply. Coming hard on the heels of an earlier crisis over Israel and Zionism, for a time it seemed possible that the future of UNESCO was in doubt. In the end a compromise was reached and the director-general, Amadou Mahtar M'Bow of Senegal, was requested to hold further consultations with experts on the declaration with a view to producing a revised, and less politically sensitive, draft for submission to the 1978 conference in Paris. A drafting committee was set up to prepare a new version, which subsequently worked in conditions of strict confidentiality. An International Commission for the Study of Communication Problems was also established by UNESCO under the chairmanship of Sean MacBride.

What emerged from the Drafting Committee in late 1977 was a document following much the same approach as earlier versions. It still called for codes of professional ethics to guide journalists in the exercise of their profession, and maintained the proposal that erroneous news reports which are prejudicial or contrary to the principles of the declaration should grant entitlement to an international right of reply for individuals, institutions or States. As in previous texts, stress was laid on the responsibility of the mass media for promoting the ideals of the declaration among young people. Although there was less emphasis on the role of the State in securing compliance by the media with the principles of the declaration, the responsibilities of the international news agencies and broadcasting organizations were particularly underscored. Behind it all lay the firm belief that it was for governments to rule what was true and what was erroneous, and that controls on the press were justified as a means of achieving political, economic or social objectives.

As statements of general principle, declarations of this sort by international bodies, particularly when they are of an unenforceable character, might seem to be unobjectionable enough. Yet over the period of time that the UNESCO draft declaration was in gestation, the disquiet of Western governments, stimulated by Western journalists and professional bodies, turned to positive opposition. The International Press Institute stated that 'Along with many governments, international organizations and individuals, we are against the draft despite its good intentions.'[10] An alarm signal went out to broadcasters from the European Broadcasting Union at a meeting of its Administrative Council held in Athens on 1 July 1978:

Considering the possible importance to broadcasting organizations of the 1978 UNESCO General Conference, the Administrative Council recommends EBU members to take the necessary steps at national level to be represented in their national delegation. As an observer at the General Conference, the Union should stress the purely professional aspects of all questions concerning broadcasting.

Confrontation became inevitable at Paris because the Third World and the West were in deep disagreement on what policies should be collectively adopted by UNESCO, a supposedly neutral body set up to serve the interests of all its 146 member states. UNESCO suffered from the same internal conflicts as the United Nations. It needed to identify with the interests of the large number of relatively poor member states which were preoccupied with development and which, apart from anything

else, had a voting majority in the Assembly. At the same time
it had to recognize the realities of power and wealth in international politics, illustrated by the fact that as much as a quarter
of the total budget of the entire organization came from a single
Western member, the United States. This financial support had
already been jeopardized by a previous controversy over
Israel's cultural policies in the occupied territories, when for
two years the United States had suspended its contribution.

At the bottom of the differences was the issue of State control.
The British delegation to the Paris Conference was led by Dame
Judith Hart, then Minister for Overseas Development. She was
forthright in stating that Britain, together with other Western
countries, was totally opposed to any wording which would
include State control of newspapers, news agencies or broadcasting. If such a declaration were adopted by UNESCO, the
British Government would have to ignore it. 'We could not
exercise those powers which the draft declaration is asking us to
exercise,' she said. Although she did not envisage Third World
countries using the declaration to control foreign journalists, as
'that would go against their declared intention of allowing the
free flow of information', there could be no question of Britain'
imposing the legislative controls envisaged.[11]

Other commentators, notably Conor Cruise O'Brien, writing
with first-hand experience of the United Nations and the
developing countries, pointed out that behind all the double
talk and verbosity lay straightforward considerations of power:

> The slogans and slogan-concepts in question have an
> intrinsic appeal to all Governments which can totally con-
> trol their own domestic flow of news, and would like to
> have as much control as they can over the international
> flow also. That is what underlies the concept of 'balance'
> in the phrase 'free and balanced flow of information' so dear
> to the heart of the UNESCO Secretariat, because so dear to
> the numerous Governments in question.[12]

The outcome of the conference was essentially yet another
compromise. Rather than risk the breaking up of UNESCO,
further changes were made in the wording of the draft declaration. Every line, every word, every punctuation mark had been

the subject of long and sometimes acrimonious controversy. The wording of the second article of the declaration was watered down so that it said only that the mass media should be 'responsive to concerns of peoples and individuals . . .' As so often the lowest common denominator had to be employed if any consensus was to be reached, and it was evident from the comments made after the declaration had eventually been passed that delegates were left in no doubt that their own governments and news media would interpret the non-binding declaration in markedly different, if not contradictory ways. An ingenious denial by a British spokesman that the final document represented a compromise was put forward on the grounds that no one had compromised their principles:

> The declaration meets our major concern. It places no hint of State control on the freedom for information to flow nor on the freedom for journalists to have access to information. These are the freedoms which in our view make democracy work.[13]

Finally, at the twentieth session of the General Conference in Paris on 22 November 1978, the draft declaration was put to the vote. It was carried by acclamation. The text is reprinted as Appendix I at the end of the book.

III

This account of UNESCO's involvement in the debate over the role of the international media demonstrates that there is more than one way of looking at the freedom of the press. Over much of the Third World, the international news media appear as alien, seldom sympathetic and often hostile. As seemingly rich and powerful outsiders, they breed suspicion and resentment.

The four leading Western news agencies are particular targets for attack. These are Reuters of Britain, the French Agence France Presse, and the Associated Press (AP) and United Press International (UPI), both of the United States. The news agencies make their own selection of what is or is not news about the developing countries, and many governments would like to see a more balanced, meaning a more favourable, picture of themselves presented to the rest of the world. One veteran observer of the international scene, Colin Legum, who is well versed in the policies and attitudes of Third World countries, has described their reasons for dissatisfaction as follows:

> First, that the Western Press, especially, distorts their position by concentrating largely on 'disaster reporting' and by giving much greater prominence to failures of policy and corruption than to the positive aspects of their societies and to their developmental needs.
>
> Second, that the flow of international news is lopsided, with most of the flow being controlled by a few major Western news agencies.
>
> Third, that they suffer from serious under-development in their own communications systems, which make it impossible for them to redress the balance.[14]

Nor do the entertainment media: films, magazines and the non-factual side of international television programming, escape criticism. Heavily American-orientated as they are in many parts of the world, they are regarded as a form of cultural imperialism: intrusive, uninvited and all-pervasive. Neither the free reporting of news events and editorial judgements made about the significance of such events, nor the unbridled enjoyment of leisure, are seen as adequate reasons why the national press and broadcasting organizations should not be mobilized in support of the purposes of the State and the planned development of its economic and social resources.

The Western nations, through boredom or irritation, should not allow the argument to go by default. It is not enough to assert that the way things are done in the West should be adopted lock, stock and barrel by those building new societies in totally different conditions. It has not always been so in the West, nor is there any natural law of universal application which declares that our way is best. What is called for is a constant and positive reiteration of the libertarian principles of which a free press is only a reflection. These should be spelt out simply and emphatically. Freedom of the press rests upon the individual's right to freedom of speech. It is a collective and systematized extension of it, enabling a citizen to address an audience rather than an individual or group of individuals. Herein lies what is regarded as the power of the press and the fear and suspicion which it so often attracts. Nevertheless it is inherent in a free society that the liberty of the individual citizen should be paramount. Freedom of speech is an essential prerequisite if there is to be informed and vigorous public debate.

Public debate should precede public decisions, and in such debate private individuals should be free to express their own opinions, subject to the restrictions set by law, without fear that dissent from the orthodoxy of the time will be punished. Apart from the benefits which follow in terms of the strength and maturity of the political society, it is only by these means that the full potential of the rational mind and the human personality, the supreme gifts which have been conferred upon mankind, can be liberated and fulfilled. Viewed in this way, freedom is not an ambiguous concept to be interpreted in the light of varying social and political circumstances. It admits of no exceptions and is, in the words of the carefully considered phraseology of the report of Sean MacBride's UNESCO Commission: 'applicable to people all over the world by virtue of their human dignity'.[15]

Some references to human rights, a term generally understood to refer to these principles, were eventually included in the final version of the 1978 UNESCO declaration, having been added largely at the instigation of the United States.[16] The wording of the declaration showed little awareness, however, that it is the political conditions in which the means of public communication operate that the touchstone of true press freedom is to be found.

Such conditions evolve, often over a long period. Democratic principles have never survived without roots, and these roots take time to get established. In the England of the sixteenth century the control of all printing presses was in the hands of the Crown and was enforced by the Court of Star Chamber. No one was permitted to print except by licence, and the exclusive right of printing was granted to the Stationers Company which came to exercise a censorship of the press and had powers to seize unauthorized publications. The system of licensing continued until 1694, having been originally imposed on all printed matter in 1530. Throughout the eighteenth century the degree of liberty varied considerably at different times. But the early newspapers and journals had one great advantage. They stood as a manifestation of a changing political climate. They grew up alongside Parliament as the authority of the Crown and the Church went into decline. Even so, Parliament and the press were rivals and it took nearly two centuries, in which a predominantly liberal climate of opinion was emerging, before the most burdensome restrictions imposed by the State on the British press were lifted.

Among the most important of these restrictions was the law on seditious libel. Once the licensing system had gone, publishers and editors risked having their premises searched and their publications seized by officials armed with warrants issued by one of the Secretaries of State. Adverse criticism of government was made more difficult by reason of the fact that, until the law was changed in the mid-nineteenth century, it was not open to a publisher to justify the publication of admittedly harmful words on the ground that they constituted a true and accurate account. Newspapers were also taxed or subsidized throughout most of the eighteenth century, and it was not until the nineteenth century that the House of Commons allowed the reporting of Parliamentary proceedings. That, too, only came about after a long and stormy argument between the politicians of the day and the publishers of journals and newspapers.

IV

If many of the justifications for a free press ultimately lead back to the need for individual freedom of expression, it is necessary to take note of the way in which newspapers, radio and television operate in a free society. It is not easy to disentangle the various strands which combine to make up the political process. But it is worth mentioning two at this stage, each of which illustrates the contemporary role of the media of mass communication. First there is the need to promote debate. Democracy depends on debate, on the clash of opinions freely expressed, and such debate requires a forum. The House of Commons is the forum for the elected Members of Parliament and the Council chamber for members of local authorities. But there is a wider public debate on the issues of the day which is conducted in the pages of daily newspapers, on radio, and on television screens throughout the country every evening. Such comment and exchanges do not decide anything, but they have an impact, particularly in determining the all-important climate of opinion within which all decisions have to be taken, whether by government or other official bodies.

The second function of newspapers and the broadcast media, which is of rather more direct political significance, lies in acting as a check on the abuse of power. Although the mass media of communication lack power, and it is right that they should, publicity itself is nonetheless a most powerful weapon. It is true, of course, that newspapers and television have considerable political influence, but they do not exercise political power in the sense of the production of intended results in the arrangements of the State.

Over and over again exposure in the press has led governments to think again. It has preserved the rights of individual citizens who might otherwise have suffered injustice; and it has caused wrong-doers to be prosecuted in the courts. Here again, as in the case of promoting public debate, the media cannot decide, and should always be wary of engaging in anything smacking of a public trial, particularly where private individuals are concerned. That must be for the institutions of the State; for Parliament which is elected; for Ministers who are answerable to Parliament; or for judges whose powers have been conferred by Statute or Common Law.

Roy Jenkins, Home Secretary at the time, dealt with some of these themes in a Granada Guildhall lecture in 1975 on 'Government, Broadcasting and the Press'. He remarked that while he was Chancellor of the Exchequer he seldom needed the press to draw to his attention the importance of particular policy issues. At the Treasury the problems of national economic policy were only too evident to all. What mattered were the solutions adopted by the government and how they were pursued. But as Home Secretary the situation was different:

In the Home Office, on the other hand, where one is dealing

to some extent with general policy but also with a multiplicity of individual cases, it is certainly true that the Secretary of State hears of some of them and applies his mind to
an attempted solution only because he reads about them in
the press, and goes into the office and asks for a detailed
report. Otherwise they would naturally, and indeed reasonably, be lost in a mass of routine which does not and cannot
in the great bulk of cases achieve Ministerial attention.[17]

The connections between a free press and personal liberty can
be seen at more than one level, and they overlap. Each individual
has a right to self-expression. He is entitled to be heard in public
if he can earn a public for what he has to say. Access to the press
and broadcasting has to be limited, by reasons of space and
time as well as by special knowledge and the ability to communicate with a wider audience. The question of accessibility to
the broadcast media is a topical one, and there are some
interesting possibilities which are discussed more fully in
Chapter 6. Nevertheless newspaper publicity and broadcast
programmes undoubtedly can and do, as Mr Jenkins has
testified, bring individual cases of hardship to the notice of those
in authority, and lead to pressure being applied in Parliament
and elsewhere for action to be taken.

The fact that it is in the public interest that there should be
effective checks on the arbitrary use of power, outside the
formal protection provided by the legal system, and outside
Parliament, has not led to a state of harmony between press and
politicians. Their relationship is one that more often has been
marked by tension and hostility. All the time, in broadcasting
as well as in newspapers, intense pressures are being brought to
bear by interested parties who fear that what is said in public on
a particular matter, or what is likely to be said, may be against
their interests. Usually, although not always, the arguments
are about political issues. Political parties in government or
Opposition, union leaders, industrialists, ambassadors and
others representing overseas interests, indeed much of official-
dom in general, is engaged in a running argument with the BBC,
the IBA and the ITV programme companies about the content,
emphasis and presentation of some part of the broadcast output.
From time to time the underlying tension erupts into a well-

publicized row. But out of public view, down below the surface, the interplay of pressure and counter-pressure is consistently at work. Nor is it any different between Fleet Street, Westminster and other centres of power.

There is nothing very sinister in this. The roles of politician and journalist are now, always have been in the past, and should continue to be in the future, quite distinct from one another. Friction is not something to be smoothed over or swept under the carpet, for it is a sure sign of a healthy democracy. Anyone who in the heat of the moment is inclined to dismiss this argument as irrelevant theorizing might be reminded of a remark made by that hard-headed old American lawyer, Oliver Wendell Holmes, who declared that the meaning of the First Amendment to the American Constitution was 'not free thought for those who agree with us, but freedom for the thought we hate'.

No one is bothered so long as the press reports and comments upon issues that are mundane or uncontroversial. Most often it is at times of crisis or communal stress when issues are of vital importance that freedom of utterance is at risk. This is why some of the most difficult and controversial of recent clashes have related to the reporting of events in Northern Ireland, or interviews with IRA or Protestant extremist leaders. Earlier, Suez and in America Vietnam, were examples of international crises where critical comment was unwelcome to government. Nonetheless it is precisely in situations of this sort that public discussion is needed most. Arthur Schlesinger, historian and White House adviser, has put it vividly: 'The cry of national unity has been used before to cut off debate and to conceal error. Democracy is not something to be suspended in an emergency.'[18]

Television, being so conspicuous, is often first in the firing line. Because it is a newer medium than newspapers, because the idea of the personal responsibility of a single editor is less clearly established, and above all because it is licensed by the State, television is particularly vulnerable to pressure, often justified in the most simplistic terms. While complaints and grievances need to be investigated and if appropriate remedied, direct pressure on broadcasters to do or not do something because it is thought it might be prejudicial to some wider interest should generally be resisted.

As with newspapers and publications, where the battle for editorial freedom was fought over a long period, so with broadcasting. There cannot be one measure of freedom for what is broadcast and another for what is printed. The whole strength of the British press in the widest sense, what used to be called rather pompously the Fourth Estate, is that it is indivisible. Since there can be no universal standard of journalistic truth, there can only be approximations of truth. These must be subjective, and the reality is that what is commonly regarded as the truth is most likely to emerge from free reporting and free discussion. A multiplicity of sources, and a multiplicity of media from which reporting and comment can originate, are the most effective counters to autocracy. Governments can govern without a free press, of course, and govern efficiently. Many do so throughout the world today. But a free press, independent of government, and capable of criticizing it if necessary, is an unmistakable mark of a free society and an important means towards achieving its ends.

V

So far the printed word and broadcasting have been discussed together as constituting the press interest in the State. This is because the basic principles which relate to freedom of the press are common to both. The time has now come in a book concerned with broadcasting in a free society to separate the two elements and to concentrate attention on the broadcast media of radio and television. Before doing so, however, and while reiterating that the case for press freedom applies over the whole range of public news media, one final comment needs to be made. It is one that is as relevant to newspapers as it is to broadcasting if complacency is to be avoided.

Important as the role of a free press is, it should not be overstated. Press proprietors have become remote and arrogant in the past, with their ears closed to all arguments that do not coincide with their own views. Editors and managements have been known to permit exhibitions of sensationalism and to encourage unwarrantable intrusions into privacy, sometimes associated with the offer of large financial inducements. Broadcast programmes, no less than newspaper articles, may contain material found by the Courts to be defamatory. If so, damages are available as a remedy. They may stray into error or even actual falsehood. If so, the programme management, or the broadcasting authorities, or both, should have the courage to apologize and if possible provide an opportunity for redress.

Editorial comment is limited on television, although it exists, and while still a frail plant it is one which is growing. I believe this to be a desirable development although it is accompanied by certain awkward problems. These relate to such questions as who should have this privileged access; should others with contrasting views be afforded similar opportunities; and how to mark the distinction between programmes of factual reporting and programmes of personal opinion. Most important of all perhaps is the problem of identity faced by the broadcaster expressing a personal view. In the same way as the columnist writing in a newspaper he is afforded a privileged vantage point, and it is one that is invariably hard-earned. He has been invited to contribute because of the strength of his opinions, and yet he cannot afford to become caught up in himself. The magnetic pull towards self-indulgence, or to put it more bluntly, pride, is very strong and very human. It should be resisted. To fulfil his obligation, and justify his position of privilege, the commentator must remain responsive to the events, the personalities and the currents of opinion that fashion the world outside the narrow confines of the newspaper office or the broadcasting studio and the febrile environments which surround them.

The fact that not everything in the day-to-day practice of journalism measures up to the resounding claims made on behalf of a free press does not invalidate its importance. When abuses occur, as they do periodically, they should be recognized and efforts made through the Press Council, the responsible managements or the broadcasting authorities, to counter them. But all the time those who are critical of the press, or who are irritated by some aspect of what appears in print or on the air, have to ask themselves whether a political system without a free press would lead to greater or less liberty for the individual citizen. There can be only one answer.

2

The Rise of Broadcasting—
and it's Conventions

I

The pre-war history of broadcasting in Britain is virtually the story of the growth of the BBC. More than almost any other national institution the BBC was a child of its time. As one of the earliest public corporations,[1] it took on a form and shape that reflected both the ideological novelties and orthodoxies prevailing in the twenties and thirties. Unlike Parliament and Parliamentary government, or the rival media of newspapers and publishing, broadcasting did not evolve over a long period of time. The BBC sprang into existence in 1927 fully fledged as a public corporation, established by Royal Charter, after only a short gestation between 1922–7. It represented a new form of organization to exploit the immense potentialities of a new technology. We take it for granted now, but the sense of wonder and amazement induced in listeners by the early wireless was caught fifty years later in a radio programme to mark the jubilee of broadcasting in 1972:

> I didn't believe them, you see; I said it was impossible for us to sit in a room and hear music, then the music wasn't there. And when they tried to say it would come through the air, well I just thought he was pulling my leg.[2]

The full story of the development of the BBC and the society in which it grew up between 1922–39 has been recounted and documented by Asa Briggs in the first two volumes of *The History of Broadcasting in the United Kingdom*.[3] Its origins go back to the formation of a limited company by a group of private wireless interests in 1922. Because of its control over wireless telegraphy, the State, in the shape of the Post Office, was involved from the outset. Thus the company was formed at the invitation of the then Postmaster-General, Mr F. C. Kellaway, and was required under the terms of a licence to provide a service 'to the reasonable satisfaction of the Postmaster-General'. Nominally the Postmaster-General was the arbiter as to what kind of matter might or might not be broadcast, but it was not long before this role was in practice assumed by the Company's strong-minded chief executive, a thirty-four-year-old Scots engineer called John Reith.[4] Reith had been originally appointed as general manager of the British Broadcasting Company, later to become the first director-general of the British Broadcasting Corporation. It was Reith's influence which was dominant in the formative years, and he left a personal stamp on broadcasting and its new institution, the BBC, for which he, more than any other individual, was responsible. A man of exceptionally strong character and temperament he was sure of one basic principle from the start: that broadcasting in Britain should be constituted and recognized as a public service, and moreover one which was independent of government control.

Reith saw to it that the use made of the new technology which permitted broadcasting by wireless was not dominated by entertainment, as had been the case in the cinema. He set his sights higher and as early as 1924, when still employed by private enterprise, he stated in robust terms:

> I think it will be admitted by all that to have exploited so great a scientific invention for the purpose and pursuit of entertainment alone would have been a prostitution of its powers and an insult to the character and intelligence of the people.[5]

The men and women Reith gathered around him firmly believed in what they regarded as the education of the public. As a result programmes that were educational in the broader sense, including talks, features, drama, music, religion and special programmes for children, were all an established part of the programme output before the first Royal Charter was granted in 1927. This Charter included a reference to 'the great value of such (broadcasting) services as means of disseminating information, education and entertainment...' a phrase that was to be repeated many times in the later history of broadcasting. As so often, these words were a formal statement of what was already happening to a large extent. Thus the precept for the future arose out of existing practice. An early pioneer, Stuart Hibberd, who joined in 1924, has recalled:

> We tried to give better and better fare to people and therefore to educate them gradually. We wanted to get people to know really good music – the classics, whether orchestral or instrumental or vocal. We put out talks and plays and broadcast really good music, which meant that if you were going to enjoy them you must sit quietly and think about them, not just to have something in the background which required no intellectual effort.[6]

For its income the BBC depended on the net revenue arising from the issue of broadcast receiving licences. These licences were permits which authorized individual householders under the terms of the Wireless Telegraphy Acts to instal and use broadcast receiving equipment in their homes. The licensing system, administered by the Post Office, was introduced in November 1922 and has endured in more or less the same form ever since. Only the cost, initially a modest ten shillings a year, has risen until at present levels[7] it has become an awkward political problem for any government to agree to make increases.

Unlike newspapers, which were dependent on circulation and advertisements for their revenue, the BBC had from the start the advantage of an independent source of finance. Members of Parliament might argue, and did so periodically, about the proportion of the licence fee which should go to the BBC, and later its level, but such matters did not require legislation. So long as the radio audience grew, as it did rapidly between 1922–39, the BBC's income grew with it. The expansion of television after the War, boosted by the introduction of colour in the late sixties, repeated the cycle over again. The problems were to come in the seventies when millions of householders to whom television and radio had come to be regarded as necessities rather than luxuries, resented the frequent increases in licence fees to finance an organization whose costs were subject to a high annual rate of inflation. This brought with it the danger that a government not satisfied with the policies of the BBC, or the decisions of its governors or management, could bring influence to bear through the power of the purse.

In the early years of expansion in the twenties and thirties, however, the BBC had the financial resources to make possible a remarkable transformation from a small private company employing no more than 371 people in 1924, to a highly regarded public corporation with an international reputation. By the outbreak of War in 1939, it was broadcasting to a national audience in over nine million homes in Britain and the staff had reached 5100. In addition the BBC had built up a significant audience overseas for its Empire Service which had been inaugurated from Daventry on 19 December 1932. Six days later came the first round-the-Empire Christmas Day programme and broadcast message by King George V.

Apart from permitting the extension of the service, adequate and stable finance also made possible a considerable measure of freedom from direct government control. Alongside the Postmaster-General's residual powers, there were a number of restrictions on editorial freedom, as well as some positive obligations such as broadcasting daily reports of the proceedings of both Houses of Parliament. News of a more general nature was restricted in the early days, information for inclusion in broadcast bulletins being originally supplied to the BBC by the news agencies in return for payment. The way this information was presented by the BBC was subject to strict limitations imposed by newspaper interests which were, rightly in the event, suspicious of the arrival on the scene of a potential competitor. After the 1927 Charter, however, the BBC began to create its own news service, as well as broadcasting eyewitness accounts of public events and commissioning talks from public men on the issues of the day.

Reith himself was generally cautious in his approach both to government and to individual politicians. No doubt he foresaw the latent rivalry that would be aroused once the political and social implications of the new medium of communication were fully realized in Westminster. In the meantime, the convention of editorial freedom for broadcasting was steadily growing. Reith in particular saw the BBC as an entity quite separate from government, operating in the public arena, and playing an increasingly important role in public life, but never controlled by Ministers.

It was an ambitious aim, but Reith had already succeeded in keeping at arm's length the commercial interests which had been responsible initially for setting up the British Broadcasting Company in 1922. He put his case to a Committee on Broadcasting appointed by the Postmaster-General in 1925 under the chairmanship of the Earl of Crawford and Balcarres and found it sympathetic to his vision of a public corporation, constituted by Royal Charter, and charged with the duty of developing a broadcasting service in the public interest. A report recommending that action be taken on these lines was published the following year.[8] Lord Crawford's committee proposed that a public commission be set up in order 'to act as a Trustee for the national interest', concluding that 'such an authority would enjoy a freedom and flexibility which a Minister of State himself could hardly exercise'. It went on to say that although 'the State through Parliament must retain the right of ultimate control . . . we think it essential that the Commission should not be subject to the continuing Ministerial guidance and direction which apply to Government Offices'.[9] The reference to the BBC's ultimate accountability being to Parliament rather than to government was fundamental, although it has remained a source of misunderstanding to the present day. Nevertheless the Crawford recommendations were accepted with little or no dissent and on 1 January 1927 the British Broadcasting Corporation came into being.

II

The advent of the BBC as an autonomous body established by Royal Charter coincided with, and probably owed something to, the exceptional events of 1926 in which broadcasting had played a significant part. While the Report of the Crawford Committee was under consideration, a matter unlikely to have been of much interest other than to a small number of people in the Post Office and the BBC, the General Strike occurred. Reith made the most of this national crisis and there can be little doubt that the BBC emerged from it stronger than before. Reith personally, and the four-year-old company he led, walked a tightrope between being identified with the government as a consequence of broadcasting a regular service of news and daily announcements, and refusing to become an instrument of official propaganda as demanded by some Ministers. In the absence of newspapers Churchill, then Chancellor of the Exchequer and temporarily editor of the official *British Gazette*, attempted to have the BBC commandeered, arguing that 'it was monstrous not to use such an instrument to the best possible advantage'.[10] Reith's reply was unambiguous. 'I told him', he wrote in his diary, 'that I was not going to have that at all.'[11] Although the BBC's constitutional position was not defined, it was a trial of strength and one that set an important precedent for the future.

Behind Reith's steadfastness lay Baldwin's support. Briggs quotes a revealing passage from Reith's diary: 'He (Baldwin) said he entirely agreed with me that it was far better to leave the BBC with a considerable measure of autonomy and independence. He was most pleasant.'[12] The fact that Reith had taken care to get onto good terms with Baldwin, and indeed had suggested the wording of part of one of the Prime Minister's broadcasts which had been delivered from his own house during the strike, underlined the desirability for the BBC to keep in with the powers that be. This was to lead to charges that the BBC was too subservient to the political establishment, and too one-sided in its coverage of the General Strike. But it must be remembered that broadcast news coverage was still in its infancy in 1926, and Reith was concerned above all to establish and preserve the right of editorial decision-making for the BBC. In moving towards this objective he was helped by the measured tone adopted in the broadcasts. The differences between the BBC coverage and Churchill's *British Gazette*, an overtly propagandist journal, stood out for all to see. In his biographical study of Churchill between 1900–39 Robert Rhodes James has observed:

> In the event, the influence exerted by the BBC was strong precisely where that of the *British Gazette* was weak; if not entirely impartial, its partiality was well concealed, and its responsible handling of news stories was in sharp contrast to the sensational approach of the *British Gazette*.[13]

At first few MPs took much notice of broadcasting. As time went on, however, and the size of the potential audience grew, licences having exceeded two million by the time of the Charter in 1927, Parliamentary interest in the wider implications of broadcasting grew with it. Broadcasting matters were debated in the House of Commons from time to time, but since the BBC had been set up as a public corporation by Royal Charter, no Minister was directly answerable for its conduct. This had been accepted by the House of Commons at the time and a statement by the then Postmaster-General, Sir William Mitchell-Thomson (later Lord Selsdon), has been repeated by successive Ministers on numerous occasions. Speaking in Parliament on 15 November 1926 he said:

> While I am prepared to take the responsibility for broad issues of policy, on minor issues and measures of domestic policy and matters of day to day control I want to leave things to the free judgement of the Corporation.[14]

Whenever questions relating to programme content or to administrative decisions taken by the BBC were raised on the floor of the House, the Postmaster-General would reply that such matters should be addressed to the broadcasting authority and not to the government. By 1929 the convention had hardened to a sufficient extent for the Speaker of the House of Commons to refuse to allow an MP to put to the Postmaster-General a question of this sort on the grounds that: 'there is no Minister who has responsibility for the British Broadcasting Corporation' and that it would be futile to put questions to Ministers on matters for which they had no responsibility.[15] When questions about the conduct of broadcasting get past the

Table today, the Home Secretary will still make it clear that such matters are primarily for the broadcasting authorities. If the Parliamentary temperature is rising he may find it prudent to add some further comment prefaced with the phrase, 'the broadcasting authorities tell me that . . .' This then opens up the subject for debate, although the Minister will usually find it necessary to remind the House that, while he will ensure that the BBC or IBA are made aware of the sentiments expressed, decisions on the content of broadcasting are properly their responsibility and not his.

By these means a subtle form of public accountability has grown up over the years. It has varied somewhat as conditions have changed, although certain underlying principles have endured throughout. First amongst these is that Ministers do not rule on what is, or is not, broadcast. Nor do they accept responsibility for what has been broadcast, or for any other controversial decisions which may have been made. This does not mean that the broadcasters are beyond control. There exist residual powers that could be used in the last resort to ban any broadcast programme, or even by withdrawal of the wireless telegraphy licence, possibly to prohibit a broadcasting organization from transmitting anything at all. In practice these drastic powers are rusty through lack of use and could only be resorted to with the consent of Parliament. No such situations have arisen in peace time during the last half-century, but that should not be taken as any sort of guarantee that they will never occur in the future.

In present circumstances what really matters is the interplay, so crucial to the working of the British political system, between public opinion and decision-taking. Parliament has constituted the broadcasting authorities and given them the job of administering and supervising the broadcasting services. The governors of the BBC and the members of the Independent Broadcasting Authority do not live and work in a vacuum. They are aware of public opinion and generally sensitive towards it. The impact of outside opinion may not always be immediately apparent, especially if, as is often the case, the opinions being expressed are divided or contradictory. Yet deep down it is the opinions prevalent in the community which shape its broadcast services. The programmes result from an amalgam of forces, some of which are explored in Chapter 4. The programme makers and the broadcasting authorities may not always be pointing in the same direction; in fact one of the most noticeable differences since the days of Reith is the absence of a sense of common purpose. But each group in its own way is responsive towards and ultimately accountable to a wider public. For Ministers to intervene directly would be not only to erode the responsibility of the people appointed on their own recommendation to represent and interpret the public interest; it would be to destroy the basis upon which that responsibility rests.

Returning to our brief survey of the political history of broadcasting, we can see that from an early stage it had become accepted that the BBC lay outside the range of direct Parliamentary control, although not beyond its influence. Nor was it thought right for the Postmaster-General, or any other Minister, to exercise day-to-day scrutiny of the programmes which were broadcast. The fact that it was the Postmaster-General who was the Minister responsible for broadcasting matters had resulted more or less from chance. Under the Wireless Telegraphy Act, 1904, the Postmaster-General's existing powers in relation to telephony, telegraphy and the transmission of telegrams were extended to include the licensing of wireless telegraphy transmitting and receiving apparatus. Such licences were charged for, both to cover administrative and regulatory costs, and to secure adequate finance to meet the cost of programmes from those who had acquired the means to receive them.

Most of the controls exercised by the Post Office were of a technical or financial nature, although the Postmaster-General himself would be expected to take an interest in the broad issues of public policy and the social implications of the new medium. In order to assist him in his consideration of these issues, and to inform and guide Parliament, the practice began of appointing from time to time independent committees to review developments in broadcasting and make recommendations for the future. The government of the day would then consider these recommendations and, having reached its own conclusions, would recommend policies to Parliament in the light of the independent findings. Successive committees of enquiry have become a regular feature of the broadcasting scene, and, although time-consuming for all concerned, they have operated as another form of public accountability by which broadcasters are periodically called upon to answer for their decisions and performance.

The first such committee was headed by Sir Frederick Sykes in 1923 and members were drawn from Parliament, the Post Office, the press, the wireless manufacturers and the BBC. Although primarily concerned with the financial problems of the BBC, then still a private company, the committee was also invited to consider broadcasting in all its aspects and to make recommendations for the future development of British broad-casting.[16] Crawford followed in 1925–6, and in the next decade, towards the end of the ten-year life authorized in the first BBC Charter, a further committee was established in 1935 under the chairmanship of a former Speaker of the House of Commons, Lord Ullswater. Its report endorsed the basic principles of the existing system and concerned itself mainly with operational problems.[17] Unlike its post-war successors the committee in 1935 reported within eight months of its establishment at a total cost to the public of £564. 10 shillings.[18]

III

As director-general of the BBC, Reith like other broadcasting executives since, was irked from time to time by having to deal with Post Office officials on matters such as financial policy when he regarded them as qualified only to handle the more technical issues such as wavelengths and transmitters. Moreover, the Postmaster-General, the political head of the department, was usually only a middle-ranking Minister outside the Cabinet. For these reasons, in the thirties the BBC hankered after a senior Minister, such as the Lord President of the Council, who normally combined political weight with Cabinet membership, assuming responsibility for the general oversight of broadcasting policy.[19] The Ullswater Committee considered a BBC proposal to this effect, but nothing came of it. There was, however, an unofficial arrangement throughout the forties, fifties and sixties by which a senior Minister, such as the Lord President, could be talked to by the BBC on very sensitive issues regarded as too 'deep' for the Postmaster-General. Herbert Morrison was one such.

Thirty years later the same arguments recurred. By then the Postmaster-General had been renamed the Minister of Posts and Telecommunications as a consequence of the Post Office being reconstituted as a public corporation in 1969. What remained of the Ministry was very small, and once again voices were to be heard arguing that responsibility for broadcasting matters should be transferred to a senior Departmental Minister with the Home Secretary as the most favoured candidate. This possibility was considered by the Conservative Administration under Mr Heath between 1970–4, but it was not until on taking office in May 1974 that the new Labour Government transferred Ministerial responsibility for broadcasting policy to the Home Secretary, then Roy Jenkins. The Ministry of Posts and Telecommunications was dissolved, with the Secretary of State for Industry assuming Ministerial responsibility for the Post Office, while the powers under the Wireless Telegraphy Acts went with broadcast policy to the Home Office. About 185 staff in all were transferred to the Home Office comprising three main departments: the Broadcasting Department, the Radio Regulatory Department and the Directorate of Radio Technology.

Until space was available in the new Home Office in Queen Anne's Gate the Broadcasting Department remained in Waterloo Bridge House in London. In this building between 1974–7 the offices formerly occupied by the Minister and his private secretary appropriately enough were made use of to accommodate the Committee on the Future of Broadcasting. This enquiry, under the chairmanship of Lord Annan, was the third post-war review. Beveridge in 1951 and Pilkington in 1962 had continued the pre-war pattern of independent public review and report before a new charter was granted to the BBC or an extended lease of life to Independent Broadcasting. Lord Annan's enquiry had first been proposed by the Labour Government at the start of the decade, and in fact Annan himself had been appointed as chairman in May 1970. However, before any members were appointed, the General Election of 1970 intervened. The new Conservative Administration dropped the idea of an enquiry at that stage, the incoming Minister of Posts and Telecommunications, Christopher Chataway, explaining that he was not persuaded of the value of launching another major enquiry. He proposed to invite the Television Advisory Committee to identify the technical questions to be studied. He said the government thanked Lord Annan, but indicated they had decided to release him from the commitment. The committee was resurrected, once more under the chairmanship of the ever patient Lord Annan, when Labour returned to office in 1974. The Report proved to be a notable contribution to public thought on broadcasting, although in the event most of its more important recommendations were not implemented. Nevertheless it was the Annan Report, and the debate it provoked, which gave shape to the discussion of public policy towards broadcasting throughout the later seventies.

One difficulty of a busy Cabinet Minister, such as the Home Secretary, in assuming responsibility for broadcasting policy is that he is already so hard-pressed with other duties that he has little time for anything except the major policy decisions. In this respect Roy Jenkins was fortunate since one of his Ministers of State at the Home Office, Lord Harris of Greenwich,[20] had considerable knowledge both of the practice and the personalities of broadcasting and was well-equipped to handle the routine business, as well as some of the prickly issues that arose. The task was a delicate one, but Harris was backed by a new and more worldly generation of senior civil servants at the Home Office, notably Robert Armstrong and Philip Woodfield.[21] Together they, and Jenkins' successor as Home Secretary, Merlyn Rees, gained the confidence of the broadcasters while pursuing the government's interests. In the aftermath of Annan, however, it seems likely that Rees and Harris were unable to persuade their Ministerial colleagues to their way of thinking, particularly their doubts about an Open Broadcasting Authority. The change of government in 1979 brought one of the most powerful Conservative Ministers, William Whitelaw, to the Home Office. With his extensive knowledge of broadcasting matters, and his influence in the Cabinet, it is unlikely that Whitelaw will encounter similar problems.

Although from time to time there may well be discord between the broadcasting organizations and the Home Office, arguments tend to relate to particular issues such as items concerning the police or prisons. Requests for intervention by other Ministers are not generally, nor should they be, channelled through the Home Office. Ministers and their advisers are well able to make their own representations, either direct or through the Chief Whip. It would be wrong to seek to draw into an argument on a particular programme the department of government which is responsible for the health and standards of broadcasting. The truth is that the broadcasters and the Home Office are in accord rather than in conflict as to their fundamental aim, namely to preserve a free and independent system of radio and television. In an article published in March 1979 while he was still an Opposition spokesman, Whitelaw stated his own position unequivocally: 'It must be the first principle of broadcasting to defend the independence of the authorities from Government and Parliament.'[22]

As we have seen, the convention of non-intervention by Ministers in the conduct of the broadcasting services goes back to the twenties. This has never prevented politicians, conscious of the need for a good press if their policies are to be implemented and their own effectiveness demonstrated, from bringing pressure to bear on the broadcasters. But in making representations, however strongly worded and however channelled, Ministers, up to and including the Prime Minister, have done so in the role of interested parties seeking to influence a decision taken elsewhere, rather than giving instructions as to what that decision must be and insisting that it is carried out. Ministerial representations are invariably listened to and urgently considered at a senior level within any broadcasting organization. It would be foolish, as well as short-sighted, to do otherwise. But the final decision lies with the relevant broadcasting authority which, as I have argued, has its own form of public accountability. It does not make for a quiet life, but it is this basic convention, more than any other, which has made possible the standards and integrity of British broadcasting in which it is right to take pride.

IV

In these often stormy seas are to be found swimming with or against the tide, the members of the broadcasting authorities, the public men and women appointed as governors of the BBC or members of the Independent Broadcasting Authority.[23] When the BBC was set up as a public corporation in 1927 the Charter provided for a chairman, vice-chairman, and three other governors to be appointed by the King in Council. In practice such appointments were made on the recommendation of the government of the day. The maximum permitted number of governors was increased from five to seven in 1937, growing to nine in 1952 and to twelve in 1968. On the latter occasion the reason for the increase in the number of governors was given as being to provide for a greater range of experience to be available. In addition to the chairman and vice-chairman the Charter specifies the designation of certain members of the governing body as national governors with particular responsibilities for Scotland, Wales and Northern Ireland. Each governor serves for a period of five years although individual governors could be, and occasionally were, reappointed for an extension.[24] While there are some variations in the structure of the Independent Broadcasting Authority, the constitutional position of the members of the authority is broadly similar to the BBC governors, except that IBA members are appointed by the Home Secretary.

Within the broadcasting organizations relationships between the BBC governors and IBA members on the one hand, and the professional broadcasting staffs on the other, have varied over the years. In the era of the BBC's first charter and licence Reith was on bad terms with the first chairman, Lord Clarendon, and also had no confidence in one of the other governors, Mrs Philip Snowden. By the time he was appointed chairman, Clarendon was already a man of some experience of public life. He had been Chief Whip in the House of Lords and Parliamentary Under-Secretary of State for Dominion Affairs, and was destined to go to South Africa as Governor-General and to serve as Lord Chamberlain of the Royal Household for fourteen years after his unhappy period at the BBC. In 1927 he lacked direct experience of administration, and had never served on a board before. The new chairman was, however, a public man, paid the then considerably salary of £3000 p.a. (equivalent to about £26,000 today), and was as anxious as Reith to do all that he could to guide the BBC down the path towards the nebulous goal of the public interest.

As it turned out Clarendon and the director-general, while not in conflict as to what the aims of the BBC should be, had totally incompatible personalities.[25] Reith, of course, was an exceptionally strong chief executive who, while accepting the need for general policy advice from the governors, clearly wanted to do things his own way. He got on quite well with Clarendon's successors, probably having learnt something from his battles with the initial chairman, although it did not prevent a later governor describing him as 'impatient, intolerant and for co-operation ill adjusted'.[26]

Once it had settled down, the role of the governors was formulated as being 'to discuss and decide upon major matters of policy and finance' but to leave 'the execution of that policy and the general administration of the service in all its branches to the Director-General and his competent officers. The governors should be able to judge of the general effect of the service upon the public, and . . . are, of course finally responsible for the conduct of it.' This description of the functions of the governors was drafted by Reith, accepted by J. H. Whitley who had followed Clarendon as chairman in 1930, and was circulated to all new governors until 1952.[27] It is a bland statement which can mean much or little, largely depending on the personalities involved and the external circumstances to which they are subject.

Two chairmen have raised the question of the role of the broadcasting authorities publicly in recent years. They provide an interesting contrast. The first, Lord Normanbrook, a former Secretary of the Cabinet, was chairman of the BBC governors between 1964–7. In a lecture on *The Functions of the BBC's Governors* in 1965[28] he gave a classic exposition of the responsibilities of those 'persons of independent mind and judgement with knowledge of public affairs' who had been selected to act as 'trustees for the national interest'. Theirs was the responsibility not only for supervising and controlling the broadcasting service, but also for 'maintaining the moral and social values which should characterize good public-service broadcasting'. The Board of Governors was 'a collective conscience' for the BBC. On the thin ice of where to draw the line between policy and execution, and the respective functions of the chairman and governors and the director-general and executive staff of the

Corporation, Normanbrook, as a veteran civil servant of wide experience, warned against the impracticability of trying to maintain clear-cut distinctions between the forming of policy and its carrying out. Constitutionally, he declared, the Board of Governors *is* the BBC: 'It is the final source of decision, not only on general policy, but on specific issues which are of sufficient importance to call for decisions at the highest level within the Corporation.'

Normanbrook's successor as chairman of the BBC governors was Lord Hill of Luton. Previously chairman of the Independent Television Authority (since 1972 known as the Independent Broadcasting Authority) Charles Hill remains the only person to have chaired both of the broadcasting authorities. Well known in two careers – as a broadcaster he had been the 'Radio Doctor' on the BBC during and after the War, and then as a Member of Parliament and a Minister, Hill had a far closer and more detailed knowledge of the politics of broadcasting than any of his predecessors. When in government he had served as Postmaster-General from 1955–7, and later had been one of the very few people to have met with any success in acting as Ministerial Co-ordinator of the government's information services. By the time he arrived at the BBC Hill, had acquired first-hand experience of the relationship between chairman, members and director-general in the broadcasting arena. Appointed as chairman of the Independent Television Authority by Mr Macmillan in 1963, soon after he had ceased to be a Minister, Hill found in Sir Robert Fraser a powerful incumbent director-general. Indeed Fraser, more than any other man, had been the architect of the system of Independent Television as it had developed since 1955. To the ITV companies, it seemed to Hill, Fraser *was* the authority: 'So Authority members were not really in authority. They were observers, watching but not contributing – and certainly not controlling. The officials, dominated by the director-general, made the decisions; Authority members acquiesced.'[29]

In the four years of Hill's chairmanship, the role of the Authority was undoubtedly strengthened, particularly since it encompassed the allocation of new franchises to the ITV companies in 1967. This critically important power to renew, alter or even terminate altogether the contracts of programme companies gives the members of the Authority a power over those responsible for programme production not shared by their counterparts on the BBC Board of Governors. Moreover, it is clearly a power to be exercised by members of the Authority rather than by the official staff who advise them. Under Hill the influence of the director-general, in this case the same man throughout (Fraser having held the appointment for fifteen years between 1954–70) was reduced and the previous independence of action which he had enjoyed was cut back. Personal relations, however, between Fraser and Hill remained cordial enough to ensure that the service of broadcasting for which they were jointly responsible did not suffer. Indeed it grew in maturity and character during the period of their partnership, uneasy though it may have been at times. This was a tribute to both men.

V

The same could not be said for Hill's initial contact with the BBC. Here once again, a strong character, Sir Hugh Greene, was already entrenched as director-general. A former journalist and broadcasting executive, Greene had been appointed director-general from within the BBC in 1960. Before Hill's advent he had served under two chairmen, one of them (Sir Arthur fforde) suffering from ill-health, the other (Lord Normanbrook) dying in office. There had consequently been periods of interregnum when a vice-chairman had presided at meetings of the governors, but the director-general effectively ran the show with little interference. Greene, however, did much more than simply exercise power as a skilful competent administrator; he had a clear idea of what the BBC should be doing in the unsettled world of the sixties and the direction in which it should move.

While the BBC's pre-war independence had been restored undiminished in 1945, a certain air of complacency had become apparent in the output and in the approach to the audience. Superimposed on this was a middle-class set of values which was rudely shattered by the advent of Independent Television in the fifties. Greene met this challenge with vigour and imagination. He left his mark on the BBC to an extent unmatched by anyone since Reith. In his book, *The Third Floor Front*, Greene recalls that on his appointment one of his colleagues was reported to have described him as a careerist with private dreams. His reply is indicative of the way he went about his task:

> I doubt whether I was ever a careerist. Things have tended to come to me in my life: I have not pursued them. But private dreams I did have and some of these dreams have been realised. I wanted to open the windows and dissipate the ivory tower stuffiness which still clung to some parts of the BBC. I wanted to encourage enterprise and the taking of risks. I wanted to make the BBC a place where talent of all sorts, however, unconventional, was recognized and nurtured, where talented people could work and, if they wished, take their talents elsewhere, sometimes coming back again to enrich the organization from which they had started. I may have thought at the beginning that I should be dragging the BBC kicking and screaming into the Sixties. But I soon learnt that some urge, some encouragement, was what all the immense reserve of youthful talent in the BBC had been waiting for, and from that moment I was part of a rapidly flowing stream. Otherwise the job could never have been done. Most of the best ideas must come from below, not from above.[30]

The appointment of Lord Hill as chairman of the BBC governors in 1967 was totally unexpected and not at all well received at the BBC. Governors and staff alike were astonished and Hill has described in his memoirs the hostile reception which awaited him at Portland Place.[31] This was partly no doubt due to the fact that he had been appointed directly from the chair of the Independent Television Authority, the BBC's principal competitor and rival. In the words of one BBC executive, it was as if Rommel had been appointed to command the Eighth Army.[32] Quite apart from the element of rebuff, no one in the BBC could be entirely sure whether the new chairman's heart still lay in ITV where he had made such a mark.

There was a second factor, to some even more disquieting. This was a suspicion that Hill had been put into the job by the

Prime Minister, Harold Wilson, in order to bring the BBC to heel. Such an emotive expression, hardly in keeping with the best traditions of a free society, was perhaps fortunately never defined. It may, and probably did, represent the feelings of frustration and anger of some of the less temperate politicians and their demand for a firmer and more politically conscious control of the BBC from the top. If that was what was expected of Lord Hill's appointment, any anticipation that the editorial freedom of the BBC would be curbed in consequence must have been quickly disappointed. It is true that as Prime Minister Wilson had personally appointed Lord Hill to the BBC chairmanship, as Heath was later to appoint Sir Michael Swann, but Hill has testified that no strings of any sort were attached to the offer. The two men had known each other for many years as political adversaries in the House of Commons and Wilson would have known that Hill could be counted on to tackle the task of the chairmanship in a more interventionist way than some of his predecessors, as he had already demonstrated at the ITA. But that was all. Nothing was asked; no undertakings were given. According to Hill's account of his interview with the Prime Minister all that happened was 'I received a straightforward invitation to take on a new job.'[33] In his own words it was an offer he found irresistible.

It was not long before the new broom brushed with Wilson who, before and after Hill's appointment, was consistently critical of the BBC's political coverage and what he regarded as its lack of fair reporting of his government's activities and achievements. Nor were the Conservatives always at one with their erstwhile Ministerial colleague, as the controversy over *The Question of Ulster* was to show. In this instance Hill and the governors supported the broadcasting of an extended television debate about Northern Ireland at a time shortly before the introduction of direct rule in 1972 when the Government had represented that such a programme could harm the already hypersensitive relations between Whitehall and Stormont.[34]

Firmness in decision-taking, however, was something the new chairman did provide. At the BBC as at the ITA before, Hill took stock and was not satisfied with what he saw. Several of the governors, he concluded, 'had become accustomed to the domination of Greene and accepted it as the way of BBC life.'[35]

Hill did not accept it and determined to change it. He wished to achieve a practice more in line with the principles enunciated by Lord Normanbrook, although not often enough implemented in his view. He pointed out that the original Whitley doctrine, built around Reith's concept of the director-general being seen to be in command, had been modified as a result of a recommendation by the Beveridge Committee which had made a comparison between the governors' functions and those of a Minister in relation to his department. No doubt to an ex-Minister, and one who had been known as a 'doer' rather than as a 'talker', this analogy may have had a particular appeal.

Hill had to move slowly at first since not all the governors were convinced that their powers, still less those of their energetic chairman, needed strengthening. After the first two years, however, when new governors had come onto the Board, and after they had collectively exercised their most important function, namely the selection of Charles Curran as director-general to succeed Sir Hugh Greene in 1969, an altered relationship began to emerge between the governors and the management. It was not just that Hill appeared to the public, and indeed to many within the BBC itself, as the head of the Corporation. It was that any major issue, whether of policy or finance, the appointment of senior staff, or the handling of controversy, came to be regarded as a proper matter for the governors or, more likely, since the governors only met fortnightly, for the chairman acting on their behalf. To some extent this situation arose from the uncertainty surrounding the appointment of a new director-general to succeed Greene which created a vacuum into which the chairman expanded. Then and later, when Curran was finding his feet, Hill secured ground probably not in any deliberate way, but because of his nature and because the ground was there to be taken by someone.

VI

It would be facile to attribute the entire change to the unexpected arrival on the BBC scene of Charles Hill and the retirement of Hugh Greene after nearly a decade's outstanding leadership. Significant though their personalities undoubtedly

were, and it is difficult to see how two such determined characters could have worked together for long, there was taking place
outside the BBC a perceptible change in the way in which public
corporations were looked upon. In the sixties and early seventies
men such as Robens at the Coal Board, Beeching at British
Rail, Ryland at the Post Office, and Melchett at the Steel Corporation, were all in the public eye. Each had a greater promi-
nence than previous mainly part-time chairmen of public
bodies, and each carried more of a public can. The institutions
they headed were, in Asa Brigg's perceptive phrase, subject to
internal strain and external attack.[36]

Broadcasting was no exception to this trend and it is evident
that Lord Hill's successor at the BBC, Sir Michael Swann, as
well as Lord Aylestone and Lady Plowden at the IBA, have all
been more involved in associating themselves with the day-to-
day affairs of the broadcasting authorities than was the case in
the past. Fundamentally this is because more is expected of
them by the public. Chairmen need to be seen to be in charge,
if they are to exercise fully and effectively on behalf of the
public the powers conferred upon the bodies over which they
preside. No chairman of a public authority can afford not to be
an interventionist today. If an MP, or the press, follow up a
controversial issue with the chairman direct, it is no use him
saying, 'That is a matter for the director-general and I will not
comment on it or do anything about it.' He is expected to stand
up in public and explain or defend what has been done, unless
the matter is clearly one of detailed administration.

Inevitably the line separating the making of policy from its
execution is one that is difficult to be precise about. It is seldom
possible to define exactly those issues which fall on one side of
the line and those which fall on the other. There are too many
imponderables. What is certain, at any rate in the short history
of broadcasting, is that the line itself has not been a static one
throughout. Matters that are regarded as properly being the
concern of the governing public authority, and those that have
been regarded as falling within the province of executive management, sometimes go one way, sometimes another. External
influences, as well as the personalities of those directly involved,
have combined with factors within the organization to bring
about these shifts in responsibility.

Quite apart from the historical significance of this ebb and flow between one group of people and another, both part of the same organization but each with a different justification for their appointments and consequent exercise of power, it is desirable that changes of this sort do take place over a period of time. If an organization, particularly a creative organization such as the BBC or Independent Broadcasting, is to be confident and flexible, adjusting itself to outside pressures and adapting itself if needs be, it must retain a degree of fluidity. Should the relationship between the appointed governors and members of the broadcasting authorities and the managements directly concerned with the supervision of the broadcast output become too prescribed or formalized, it will not be long before a climate results which is not conducive to good broadcasting.

Of course there have to be procedures and definitions, financial and production disciplines, as well as rules and guidelines on programme content and scheduling. No organization can work without them. A degree of detachment and experience obtained outside the organization is helpful in drawing these up. Always there is a need to guard against over-rigid systems, and towards spending too much time and care in attempting to define the indefinable. Instinct and judgement are invariably better guides than didacticism. In broadcasting as elsewhere the bureaucracy will gain in strength, as well as in numbers, unless positive steps are continuously taken to counter it.

To producers, the chairman, governors and members of the broadcasting authorities often seem remote and lacking in understanding of their aims and methods. Yet, as many past controversies have shown, these authorities act as a useful buffer or shock absorber between government and programme makers. This has helped to protect producers from the more extreme forms of political pressure. In practice the handling of most of the more serious incidents has been assumed by those who have a two-fold responsibility; answerability to the public on whose behalf they have been appointed, and loyalty towards the people within their own organization who have the all-important task of producing the programmes. It is an exceptionally difficult and very English horse to ride, but the very emergence of the animal has been one of the successes of the way in which broadcasting has evolved in this country. It has resulted in a range and quality of programming that is as great as any to be found elsewhere in the world.

VII

An awareness of these considerations of quasi-public policy has been present throughout the years of growth of British broadcasting. In the early stages, first in radio, then in television the organizations were small and intimate. The people working in them were mainly young, enthusiastic and generally enjoying themselves hugely. In the case of the BBC there was a strong overtone of public service. The pattern recurred again with the setting up of local radio stations in the seventies. To be involved at the start of any new enterprise, particularly one that was to grow so rapidly and have such an impact as broadcasting, was undeniably a privilege for all concerned and an experience to be looked back upon with some pride as well as pleasure.

Now the scale of broadcasting has changed. It has become an industry, and indeed is sometimes referred to as such. The BBC, with two national television channels, four radio networks as well as the national radio services in Scotland, Wales and Northern Ireland and twenty local radio stations, together with the External Services, employs some 26,600 people. The IBA, the controlling authority for Independent Broadcasting, is also responsible for the technicalities of transmitting the programmes and has a staff of about 1200. Then there are fifteen ITV programme companies, regionally based, and Independent Television News (ITN) which provides them with a service of national and international news. Finally independent local radio (ILR) is a booming growth area. Nineteen stations were in operation at the end of 1979, with an additional nine locations authorized by the Labour Government in October 1978. This was followed by a further fourteen or fifteen locations announced by the Conservative Home Secretary in November 1979. Franchises are advertised for each of these locations by the IBA and contracts entered into with the successful applicant. When the current ILR expansion programme is complete it is expected there will be a network of forty-three local radio stations throughout the country, each financed by advertising and controlled by the IBA. The BBC also has authorization to expand its local radio coverage, but shortage of money has slowed down its plans.

The greatly enlarged size and range of broadcasting organizations has brought with it problems of internal communication and control that are by no means unique to broadcasting, although they were unknown in the early days. Trade-union power has come to have a profound effect, and not only in relation to terms and conditions of employment. Attitudes towards authority and decision-making have changed markedly so that the professionalism of the programme maker: the producer or director, the writer or technician, is often set against the statutory or contractual responsibilities of the governors and members of the broadcasting authorities or their managements. At the same time there is a clear demand for more evident public accountability than in the past. So it is a different outlook, and one that reflects many of the currents that have troubled the surface of British society over the last thirty years.

Behind all the changes in the way broadcast programmes are produced and controlled, however, lie the same conventions, assumptions largely unchanged since the days of Reith. Television and radio programmes are not controlled by government or by the political parties. Politicians can and do exercise pressure, as do other groups in society. Nevertheless when in office both major parties have consistently refrained from intervening in the conduct of broadcasting. The reserve powers remain for possible use in extreme situations, but they are so draconian it is unlikely that any government would fall back on them unless it was assured of a majority in Parliament for such action. A further sanction is that under the terms of its Licence the BBC is empowered to announce that a notice has been served by the Home Secretary on the Corporation to refrain from broadcasting certain items. There is thus little opportunity for dirty work behind the scenes. Equally important is the realization that if one party in government were to resort to its ultimate powers to require material to be broadcast or suppressed in its own interest, the Opposition party could reply in kind when it came to office.

At the root of the matter lies a shared appreciation that a politically independent system of broadcasting is an essential element in a free society. It is not so in many parts of the world and it should not be taken for granted here. It is a frail plant in shallow soil. If the relative equilibrium of our political society were to change, and the fundamental freedoms of the citizen were threatened, a free press and system of broadcasting would also be threatened. But at the same time they would be powerful weapons against any potential usurpers of constitutional power.

3

Competition: Then and Now

I

Thus far the references to the BBC and Independent Broadcasting have been in parallel: a shared interest in freedom of expression; the similarity in the way in which public men and women act as members of the Board of Governors of the BBC or the Independent Broadcasting Authority; the fluctuating relationship between the chairmen and members of the regulatory bodies on the one hand and the full-time broadcasting executives on the other; the desire to keep on terms with government and Opposition, but to do so in such a way that individual freedom of speech is not compromised. Viewed in this perspective it is possible to make general statements about the 'broadcasters' which apply equally to BBC and to Independent Broadcasting. Ever since 1954, however, when the BBC's monopoly was brought to an end by Act of Parliament there has been another way of looking at broadcasting.

This has been to scrutinize the development of BBC and Independent Broadcasting as rival organizations simultaneously engaged in trying to attract and hold the attention of the individual viewer or listener at home. It is this feature more than any other which distinguishes the viewer or listener from readers of the printed media of communication: books, newspapers, journals and other publications. Although each in sum constitutes a mass audience, and hence the graceless but expressive description 'mass media', the essential difference is that the individual viewer or listener can only view or listen to one programme at a time. The increasing availability of recording and play-back devices, such as video and audio cassettes as well as the promise of video discs, may alter this situation in the future. But until it does, each broadcast programme can only be received at the time it is broadcast. It cannot, as can the book and newspaper, be put on one side for later reference.

In the case of television there is a further significant characteristic of the broadcast audience; namely that in a majority of homes there is only one TV set, whereas on average three people in the household are available and usually anxious to watch television. Hours of viewing are long; each set is turned on for an average of more than five hours a day, while individuals on average watch television for almost three hours a day.[1] Compromises have to be reached about what programme will be viewed. These vary by time of day: housewives and children tend to control the switch during most of the daytime hours, with the breadwinner returning home seeking to exert his authority in the evening. Many studies have been carried out on the factors determining viewing preferences and the way in which decisions are arrived at on what to view in the single-set home. Generally speaking the findings of a large body of behavioural research, not all of it showing the family as a unit in the best light, can be summed up in the phrase: 'No one has to watch what they hate.' Consequently it is often second choices which predominate.

It is self-evident that a wider choice can be obtained if there is more than one set available in the home. But television sets, particularly those capable of receiving colour, remain expensive items. As the market for second-hand black-and-white sets has diminished it is reasonable to suppose that a growing proportion of viewers have retained their old set when buying or renting a new colour set, thus becoming a multi-set home in the process. Whether it is because of this factor, or because more young people are buying a TV from their earnings while still living at home, there has been a marked increase over recent years in the number of homes containing more than one television set. Whereas in 1972 it was estimated that only 3 per cent of households had more than one set, by 1975 the figure had risen to 6 per cent, reaching 12 per cent by April 1978 and 16 per cent a year later.[2] In America the rise has been even sharper, so that now approximately half the total number of households in the

United States are multi-TV set homes. In Chapter 6 I note the social implications of this trend for the future and its likely impact on programming.

In Britain the widening opportunity for television viewing within the home has coincided with a counter-trend moving in the opposite direction. Over much the same period the circulations of most daily and Sunday national newspapers have declined, part of the fall being due to the cancellation of a second newspaper in many households. This is another example of how the printed and electronic media constantly interrelate with each other, with technological developments and economic factors playing as large a part as editorial rivalries.

Competition for the attention of the individual viewer was intrinsic from the start of Independent Television. Most of the people in charge of the BBC at the time recognized – although in some instances only belatedly – that a separate service, answerable to a new authority set up by Parliament for the purpose and charged with providing television programmes additional to those provided by the BBC, would inevitably alter the practice of television broadcasting. Hitherto the BBC had exercised what could fairly be described as a benevolent monopoly. Enthusiastic producers did their best with limited resources, technical as well as financial, while ultimate control of policy, including the all-important question of the rate at which the television service was developed, remained firmly in the hands of the senior management at Broadcasting House. Their preoccupation was still overwhelmingly with radio.

Short-sighted though it may appear in retrospect, the statistics show why this should have been so. In 1948 more than eleven million households were licensed to receive radio broadcasts, while only 45,564 homes in the more affluent areas of London, the South East and the Midlands had a combined licence to receive television transmissions as well as radio broadcasts. Moreover, because television sets were still a novelty they were expensive, and consequently ownership was largely confined to the well-to-do.

Programming reflected this: the Oxford vs Cambridge Boat race, Wimbledon and Lords were the venues of the earliest television sports events, rather than football matches or race meetings. Although by 1953 the audience was greatly enlarged, having more than doubled itself in each of the previous three years with combined licences exceeding two million for the first time in that year,[3] programmes were conceived with little knowledge of how they were received by the audience. Initially this did not matter, since both the broadcasters and their audience were members of the same elite. Instinct and personal taste were sure enough guides. As television began its rapid growth, accelerated by the successful coverage of the Coronation in June 1953, it embarked upon a remarkable transition from the part-time occupation of a minority of leisured people to become an integral part of the life of virtually the entire population. Today with about 23 million sets in use, 98 per cent of all homes in Britain contain a TV set and 'watching television' far outstrips all other pastimes save sleep and work. For good or ill it is a twentieth-century phenomenon which has had a profound effect on the way in which people look at the society of which they are part and hence at its nature and goals.

II

The seeds of the transformation were present in the mid-1950s. Some people in the BBC saw this clearly enough. Notable amongst them was Norman Collins, first Controller of BBC Television, who resigned in 1950 to campaign for a competitive service of television to be financed from advertising. When the challenge came, the BBC as a corporate body, one of the pillars of the establishment, had not taken seriously enough the changes that were occurring in the popular culture and the pivotal role that television was to play. Sir William Haley, no friend of television, although one of the greatest journalist/administrators of his age, had departed as director-general in 1952 to be replaced by Sir Ian Jacob, a former head of the BBC's External Services and war-time Military Assistant Secretary to the Cabinet. A retired Permanent Head of the Foreign Office, Sir Alexander Cadogan, was chairman of the governors. When the storm broke and the Popular Television Association, backed by sections of the Conservative Party and certain business interests, launched its attack on the BBC monopoly, the BBC had no difficulty in enrolling the support of an overwhelming majority of the great and the good. Archbishops, peers, vice-chancellors had little hesitation in denouncing the idea of commercial television. Lady Violet Bonham Carter agreed to take the chair of a newly formed council to resist its introduction.

Undoubtedly many opponents were influenced by the adverse effects of sponsorship which had been evident in the United States, although few had studied the differences between America, where broadcasting was, and always had been, primarily conducted as a business to maximize profit, and what was being advocated for Britain. The essence of the proposals which evolved from discussions between the interested groups and the Conservative Government was that only a limited amount of time, about 10 per cent, could be occupied by advertisements, and that these advertisements must be seen to be distinct from the programmes. When it finally went on the statute book the Television Act, 1954 was specific on this point; the Second Schedule to the Act stating, 'The advertisements must be clearly distinguishable as such and recognizably separate from the rest of the programme.'[4] Thus from the start of the new service of television a mechanism was introduced to prevent the sponsorship of programmes by advertisers, and the control of programme content that goes with it. Moreover once ITV began, not only were the so-called spot advertisements, usually of between fifteen and sixty seconds in duration, kept distinct from the programmes, but the staffs concerned with the sale of advertisement time were deliberately insulated from the programme departments. As a result it was not long before most of the heat went out of the argument over sponsorship.

It was hardly surprising that the weight of authority was aligned with the BBC against its would-be competitor. Not only did the BBC have a high reputation for editorial integrity, mainly earned in sound broadcasting, but its contributions to the cultural life of the nation, especially in music and drama, were widely admired. Moreover, television, then as now, was little watched by busy professional middle-class people with many other things to do. Also present in the early years was a sort of fashionable snobbishness which inferred that television was somehow rather contemptible and the TV set was worthy only of a place in the servants' hall. Most of the newspaper magnates and cinema owners were also opposed to the introduction

of a service of television financed by advertising, with
the exception of the populist *Daily Mirror.* A defensive reaction
was to be expected since both were highly interested parties
whose businesses were likely to suffer from a new competitor
entering the same market place. Later almost all changed their
tactics and by the time ITV was launched several newspapers
and cinema groups were represented in the shareholdings of the
first companies to be granted programme contracts, while
others had shown an interest in taking part.

A very different opponent was to be found in the Labour
Party. Herbert Morrison, who as Lord President of the Council
had played an important part in post-war broadcasting policy,
was the key figure. To Morrison, always very close to Parliamentary opinion, the fact that a number of Conservative backbenchers were actively associated with the campaign to end the
BBC's monopoly was enough to persuade him that the Tories
were out to curb the power of the BBC, which he prided as one
of the most successful public corporations, and were ready to
hand over valuable public resources to their friends in big
business. In Parliamentary debate Morrison was able to call in
aid the recommendations of the Broadcasting Committee under
Lord Beveridge which had reported early in 1951.[5] This committee had been set up by the Labour Government in 1949, and
Morrison himself had invited Beveridge to take the chair. The
committee recommended that all forms of broadcasting, television and the overseas services as well as sound radio, should
continue to be provided by the BBC. One member, however,
dissented. In a minority report Selwyn Lloyd, at the time an
up-and-coming backbench Conservative MP, argued for an end
to the BBC monopoly and favoured the introduction of both
commercial radio and commercial television. Finally, after
much discussion and a change of government, it was to be this
view that prevailed.

As was to happen again a quarter of a century later with the
report of the Annan Committee, the Labour Government was
in no rush to bring proposals before Parliament to implement
Beveridge's recommendations or any variations of them. Instead
it encouraged a period of public debate and comment. There
was little change in the reasons between the early fifties and the
late seventies. Broadcasting policy is a matter of consuming

interest only to a handful of MPs on either side of the House. Some of them have first-hand experience of broadcasting and feel strongly about it. They debate, write and lobby keenly and forcefully, and generally play a conspicuous part in the public discussion of current issues concerning broadcasting and of future policy. To the majority of MPs of all parties, however, broadcasting is little more than one of the means by which they can make themselves and their views known to their constituents and to a wider public on other matters. Consequently broadcasting legislation seldom has had a high place on the Parliamentary or legislative agendas. Governments have many other more urgent preoccupations and Ministers and civil servants have usually sought to find a measure of common ground in their approach. In determining what is common ground the prevailing public mood is a critical factor.

III

In 1954 the public mood was very different from the late forties when Beveridge had begun his inquiry. War-time controls, which had been continued after the end of the war because of shortages of food and materials, had been scrapped. The economy was beginning to speed up, more houses were being built, and a wider range of goods was becoming available to the consumer in the shops. R. A. Butler was Chancellor of the Exchequer and he has recorded in his memoirs the situation as he saw it in preparing his 1954 Budget:

Nearly all State trade had been given back to private enterprise. Competition had been restored in the steel and road haulage industries. Most price controls were abolished. Thousands of controls on the allocation of materials and the manufacture and sale of goods were removed. Import controls had been greatly relaxed. The great commodity markets had been re-opened. Above all, food rationing and other restrictions on consumption had been brought to an end.[6]

In retrospect the mid-fifties stand out as the high watermark reached by capitalism since 1945. Later as economic management became fashionable, and as its limitations began to appear, disillusion set in. But in 1954 there was a sense of confidence and experiment in the air. Investment was once again possible, financial risks could be taken, and profits made. More and more people were asking why all broadcasting had to be controlled by a single corporation when there was a multiplicity of newspapers, national and regional, competing with one another. Businessmen were not alone in putting this question. The *Economist*, for example, consistently argued against the BBC monopoly on grounds of principle. Former employees pointed out that those who fell out with the Corporation had nowhere else to go to practice their craft and earn their living. BBC programme standards were competent, and the engineering excellent, even if the coverage of politics and outside sporting events was still very restricted.

The effect of competition on programme standards, particularly if financed by advertising, was impossible to quantify and yet it was this factor more than any other which was placed in the forefront of debate by the supporters of the public monopoly. Central though the argument undoubtedly was, and powerful the advocacy by such stalwart BBC supporters as Lord Halifax, Lady Violet Bonham Carter and Christopher Mayhew,[7] it was nevertheless impossible to establish one way or the other to general satisfaction whether the programmes would be improved or debased by competition. As the public debate went on it became clear that there was no common vocabulary on which to make judgements as to what constituted improvement and what marked deterioration. The flavour of the controversy was neatly captured by the *Economist* which remarked, 'In that subtle way that is unique to this Island, it is not so much stated as taken for self-evident that only cads would want to have advertising on the air.'[8]

The tone adopted in the debate by most of the opponents of competitive television, including the Labour Party's publicity,[9] left an impression that if it remained in sole possession of the field at the end of the day the BBC might settle for a somewhat high-minded and patronizing approach to its audience. A. J. P. Taylor, writing in the *New Statesman* in 1961, claimed:

To this day, the high-minded defenders of the BBC monopoly do not understand what hit them. They think it must
have been some sinister conspiracy. Yet the real explanation is simple: many people were growing to dislike the rule
of the high-minded . . . Why should viewers be denied
programmes which they enjoyed, and be given programmes
only which did them good? This question was dynamite.
Once asked, there was no effective answer.[10]

Feelings of this sort coincided with some strongly voiced
criticism that the top management of the BBC had not been
sufficiently interested in encouraging the full potential of television and had held it back. That the development of the new
medium had been inhibited was undeniable. Why this should
have been so is harder to explain. No doubt problems over the
allocation of scarce resources loomed large in the minds of the
BBC's governors and senior management. Yet Haley, in particular, was a far-sighted man and there is no indication that he
saw any need to give priority to the expansion of television.
Despite its limited audience television attracted much attention
and interest in the press, and as events turned out, the press
proved to be a better judge of the public pulse than the BBC
governors or management. To Haley, as to many others inside
and outside the BBC, especially in public life and in Parliament,
all this smacked of novelty, in no way comparable with the solid
achievement of sound radio. Norman Collins later recalled:

To keep things in perspective it is important to remember
the public esteem in which the BBC was held because of its
magnificent wartime record in sound broadcasting. Though
television had seized the popular imagination it was – not
least in parliament – regarded as little more than an ingenious novelty. Indeed, a leading member of Mr Attlee's
cabinet described it to me as 'nothing more than a rich
man's toy'.[11]

These were the main factors which combined, causing the
bandwagon for competitive television to begin to roll. The
campaign was backed by some business interests which stood
to gain, although few businessmen were convinced of it at the

time and in fact substantial financial losses were incurred in the
first phase of ITV. It was also significant that the issue became
so quickly politicized. This was partly a consequence of the
activities of an energetic group of younger backbenchers on the
Conservative side of the House of Commons. They were encouraged by Mark Chapman-Walker, the Chief Publicity Officer
at the Conservative Central Office. Chapman-Walker was close
to Collins and his backers, and also had the ear of Lord Woolton,
the Party chairman, whose influence was critical when the
government came to decide. Equally important, on the other
side of the political divide, was the decision of the Labour
leadership to oppose the introduction of commercial television.
It was this decision more than any other, probably reached
intuitively rather than on the basis of any careful thought,
which polarized the controversy and translated it into an issue
between the two main parties in Parliament.

In *The History of Broadcasting in the United Kingdom*, Asa
Briggs notes a statement made by Attlee in June 1953 that if a
Conservative Government 'handed over television to private
enterprise' Labour would 'have to alter it when we get back
into power'.[12] Thereafter Conservative opinion was consolidated and the Whips were on. This declaration, and Morrison's
Parliamentary tactics, represented a classic instance of an
Opposition making the case against its own interests. Without
their intervention the die was by no means cast since several of
the most powerful Conservative Ministers including Churchill,
Eden and Butler, were still doubtful and had been wary of
appearing to fall in too readily with the aims of an evidently
well-organized and vocal pressure group. Nevertheless, they
were aware that the anti-monopolists on their own backbenches
represented an authentic feeling at the grass roots.

The eventual outcome was a compromise, although one that
went against the BBC and its supporters. The legislation which
was introduced in 1954 authorized an alternative system of
television that was to be financed by the sale of advertisement
time. The amount and type of advertising was to be regulated
by a new authority, to be known as the Independent Television
Authority (ITA), as would be the programmes. These were to
be provided by a number of contracting companies, separate
from each other as to finance and control, which would be

licenced by the authority. In this way Parliament, mediating between conflicting interests, reached a reconciliation between the claims of free enterprise and the claims of the State to regulate what was generally regarded as a public resource, namely the broadcast wavelengths. It may have been a long-drawn-out episode, and some of the debate had certainly been noisy and acrimonious. Yet when all was said and done, it was a striking example of the way in which Parliamentary democracy could perform its task in the post-war world. Party political considerations, Parliamentary opinion, personal ambition, business and financial interests, and organized pressure groups all reacted with one another. It is not possible to say that any one element predominated.

An American observer, Professor H. H. Wilson, was later to conclude that commercial television came about in Britain largely as a result of the work of a small but well-funded pressure group.[13] As an explanation this is too simplistic. Although the Popular Television Association undoubtedly played an important part, as did its adversary the National Television Council, neither body decided the issue. It was eventually resolved in Parliament and by Parliament.

Nor was this an instance of a monolithic government or party machine deciding on what it wanted to do and then forcing a measure through the legislature. Professor Wilson's thesis, curious for an American since public opinion is often more highly regarded in the United States than here, is no more than history in a single perspective. It attributes too much to direct cause and effect and not enough to the underlying spirit of the time. In 1954 a current was flowing strongly in the tide of public opinion. There were, of course, cross-currents; for popular opinion is seldom unified. It was the anti-monopoly, anti-highminded, anti-'them up there' current which came to the surface and prevailed. Perhaps the early stirrings of the iconoclasm and dissent that was to mark the sixties were beginning to show through. But no detectable symptoms of autocracy were apparent in the process.

The way in which the BBC's entrenched monopoly position was terminated was, to some at least, heartening evidence that Paraliment stood not just as a traditional monument to a free society, but as an institution capable of furthering its ends. In acting the way it did on this issue Parliament lived up to its own supreme role. This has been well described by one of its staunchest champions, Enoch Powell, as the representation of the nation, not only in terms of locality, but as 'representation for the purpose of saying yea or nay. It is not an attempt to find out the exact shadings of opinion across the whole spectrum. It is a means of arriving at valid, sustainable decisions.'[14]

IV

The competitive system which resulted has endured ever since. ITV has changed as the BBC has changed over the years in response to the evolving environment within which both broadcasting services are contained. In its essentials, however, Independent Television today still corresponds closely with the blueprint laid down in the Television Act of 1954. In the language employed by Mr Powell, albeit speaking in another context, it has turned out to be 'a valid sustainable decision'. Competition has not pleased everyone, but that ITV has provided pleasure for many millions is self-evident. In the years that followed, Independent Television grew into a national institution. Its relationship with the BBC matured. Its international reputation grew. Politicians liked its regional structure with the additional opportunities it provided for political communication. Civil servants – particularly in the Treasury – liked the fact that ITV financed itself from advertising and did not require the imposition of taxes or the raising of additional revenues by way of licence fees. Indeed as it became profitable it contributed many millions to the Treasury from a special levy on profits. Above all, over the years Independent Television was to make possible the production of innumerable programmes of skill and imagination, of political integrity and independence. Critics there have always been and it is desirable that their voices should be raised and heeded. They are the principal antidote to complacency, one of the deadly sins of broadcasting, as it is of any other creative activity. But the achievements of Independent Television are there, and they should not be minimized.

For the social historian of the future one of the most interesting aspects of the development of ITV since 1954 will be the manner in which it took on a noticeably regional identity. In 1979, when introducing the Independent Broadcasting Authority's plans for public participation in the process leading up to decisions on future contracts, the director-general, Sir Brian Young, was able to assert without fear of contradiction:

> Everyone knows that ITV is a mosaic. Fifteen companies give a network of programmes seen nationally and a number of local services, of a particular pattern that varies from place to place and appeals strongly to regional loyalty.[15]

ITV was not, however, conceived as a mosaic, nor as a regional service. It was set up, as we have seen, as an alternative national system of television by Act of Parliament in order to compete with the BBC. No doubt it was expected that the new service, in the same way as the BBC, would establish regional outposts and aim to reflect the life and work of the various regions of the United Kingdom as far as possible in its programmes. The characteristic regional character of ITV which was to emerge goes back not to any decisions of public policy before its inception, but to the way in which it was organized in the early years.

The form of organization which was adopted resulted from a novel approach. Subsequently regionalism in broadcasting became associated with the growing demand for devolution. But in the fifties the Independent Television Authority was in advance of contemporary public thought in the way it approached the task of organizing the new service of television which had been entrusted to its care by Parliament. Sir Robert Fraser, director-general for the first fifteen years, and as already mentioned a man with a better claim than any other to be regarded as the architect of the system of ITV as we know it today, has described what was in the Authority's mind at the time:

> It had seemed to the Authority in 1955 that one thing in Britain beginning to go wrong was the over-concentration of the control, ownership and direction of the means of communication; a process which had reached its absolute

extreme in the BBC, the only permitted agency of broadcasting in the country, an agency of the State, and national-
ized. The Authority therefore thought it wise to carry as far
as the economy of ITV would allow the principle of dis-
persion and pluralisation . . . The second major formative
principle behind the present ITV system had been the
Authority's belief in the value of the separate communities
that make up the United Kingdom as a whole, distinctive,
recognisable regional communities.[16]

This latter factor was a consequence of trying to arrange for
separate companies to broadcast on a single channel, and for
some of them to provide programmes for a nationally networked
service. Had a second channel been available to ITV from the
outset, the story of regionalism on British television might well
have been very different. Earlier in the same address from which
the above quotation is drawn, Fraser had speculated on the
institutional arrangements that would have followed. He con-
jectured that two directly competitive seven-day companies
would have been established in London, each being responsible
for its own service of network programmes. These programmes
would then be supplied to a number of subsidiary regional
stations operating outside London; two each in the major areas
of population; and one each in the smaller areas which for
economic reasons could not support two.

The result would have been a largely centralized, largely
unitary production of network programmes, planned and produced by one company and distributed to affiliates over the rest
of the country. There would probably have been room for the
syndication of programmes produced by independent producers,
and there would certainly have been programmes of local
interest produced by the regional stations. In effect, according
to Fraser, each regional company would have decided from
which London source to draw its network programmes, to what
extent to transmit programmes acquired through syndication,
and to what extent to produce its own local programmes. Such
a system, he concluded:

. . . would have been clear and logical, relatively easy to
operate, and much closer to that of other television

organisations. It did not come about, of course, because it was possible to introduce only one service. The arrangements that in the event were made for the supply of network programmes would strike the foreign observer as both strange and cumbrous.[17]

The description 'strange and cumbrous' is well chosen and it is one that still applies. Few foreign observers, or for that matter those closer to home, find the organization and working of ITV easy to understand, although many overseas broadcasting systems have adopted the device of obtaining revenue from advertising in order to meet the ever-increasing costs of television production. It has been demonstrated that advertising can be separated effectively from the programmes, and that guidelines can be laid down and enforced by a public authority to ensure that responsible practices are observed. It is now a fact that every country in Western Europe, save only Belgium, permits some kind of advertising in its television service. Most European broadcasters regard the practice that has grown up as flexible and effective, depending, as is the British way, more on common understandings than on codes and edicts. It also provides a method of obtaining finance for broadcasting other than from public funds, while avoiding the dangers of the American model where the idea of sponsorship is deeply engrained.

There is an irony that at a time when sponsorship, for so long regarded as the bugbear of commercial broadcasting in Britain, should finally and laboriously have been laid to rest, attempts should have been made to resurrect it by, of all people, the advocates of an Open Broadcasting Authority. This recommendation by the Annan Committee found some support in the Labour Administration and Parliamentary Party before the 1979 General Election, but since then the fourth channel has been allocated by the Conservative Government to the Independent Broadcasting Authority. This body, formerly the ITA, but renamed when responsibility for independent local radio was added in 1972, has already made it clear that the new channel must have adequate financial support if it is to succeed in its aims. Sponsorship, although superficially attractive in that it is less conspicuous than a series of advertisements, and sometimes provides revenue from different sources, is nonetheless an insidious and dangerous basis for any broadcasting system.

However reasonable and public-spirited the sponsoring organization, and some of the largest American corporations have shown themselves ready to sponsor outstanding programmes on American television, they are not in the business of upsetting people. To the sponsor any controversy is suspect – not just in news and documentaries, but in drama, entertainment, even religious programmes. It seems hard to credit, but General Motors withdrew from the sponsorship of Franco Zeffirelli's epic *Jesus of Nazareth* on the NBC Television Network because of protests made to automobile dealers by Southern Baptists. Neither protestors nor sponsor had in fact seen the film which at the time was unfinished. But some remarks by Zeffirelli reported in the press as to how he saw the subject were enough. The story had a happy ending in that another sponsor was found and the entire film was shown by NBC, and later repeated, being received with acclaim. If this example is thought to be too far-fetched and remote from British practice one need look no further than the BBC's experience with grants from local authorities when local radio was first set up in the sixties. This is described in Chapter 5. Limited sponsorship of sporting or artistic events may be acceptable in certain circumstances, but as a wider method of financing a broadcasting service sponsorship is open to many objections.

Sir Robert Fraser's reference to a system that was 'strange and cumbrous' arose from the arrangements which have evolved over the years for the supply of network programmes, rather than the way ITV is financed or the advertising interests kept at arm's length. It is a system hardly known outside ITV, although the procedures were investigated and in the main accepted by Lord Annan's Committee on the Future of Broadcasting.[18] What happens is that the five companies operating in what are known as the central areas: ATV, Granada, London Weekend, Thames and Yorkshire, have the responsibility of providing a range of programmes every week which are suitable for national audiences. It is specified in their contracts with the IBA that they should do so. The number of programmes produced by each company in various categories – drama, entertainment programmes, current affairs, sport, education, religious programmes and so on – is related to its net advertising revenue. These programmes are exchanged by the central companies so that they can be seen in each other's areas and jointly offered in return for a fixed annual payment as a guaranteed weekly network supply to the other ten regional companies.

This guaranteed network supply includes virtually all of the best known programmes of ITV which, together with film material which is also acquired on a network basis, occupies the peak viewing hours between 6.30 p.m.–10.00 p.m. every weekday evening, with the main national and international news following at ten o'clock. Programmes such as Anglia's natural history series *Survival*, Southern's programmes for children, and occasional drama series like Scottish Television's *The Prime of Miss Jean Brodie* are also networked, once accepted for national screening by the Network Programme Committee. The timing of showings may vary from one region to another, but basically the network service is what most viewers regard as being the mainstream of ITV.

V

It ought to be emphasized that each network programme is planned and produced by an ITV company with a separate identity. The Programme Controllers of the five central companies meet weekly with the IBA's Director of Television and the Director of the Programme Planning Secretariat, who takes the chair. This meeting is, however, primarily concerned with scheduling; not with commissioning or supervising production. Consequently different companies, with differing producers and directors working with separate programme managements, have formed distinctive styles. These varying styles are a source of vitality and strength to Independent Television as a whole, and were recognized as such in the Annan report.[19] The ideas come from specialist programme staffs within companies or from freelancers, particularly writers and directors, who offer their work, often through agents, to the BBC or ITV companies. Annan also accepted a proposition that had been put to the committee by a producer experienced in both ITV and BBC, Jeremy Isaacs, that there was more strength, justice and flexibility in a system where a programme suggestion offered to the ITV network was rejected or accepted by a group of several people than being left to the fiat of the Controllers of BBC 1 or BBC 2.

As a result of the differing attitudes of the individual programme Controllers, and the collective outlook of the producers they represent, the five central companies are able to concentrate their resources on alternative priorities. For example, while Granada may have been concentrating on the *State of the Nation*, or London Weekend on the problems of entertainment programming for family audiences on Saturday evenings, ATV has been seeking to develop a style of more personalized film-making by directors of the calibre of Antony Thomas, Brian Moser and Adrian Cowell. Very substantial sums are spent on the direct costs of programming for the network each year, while the indirect costs, that is the cost of studios and the permanent production staff and facilities, are even higher. Expenditure on this scale is made possible only by the size of the contract areas allocated by the IBA to the central companies. These vary between a total population of about seven million people in the Yorkshire Television area, and not far short of fourteen million in the London area. The franchise to broadcast in the London area, because of the size of its audience and its potential dominance, has been split between two companies ever since the start of Independent Television.

The regional functions of the ITV companies, large and small, important as they are, need to be seen against the background of the network service. This is what ITV means to many millions of people throughout the United Kingdom. Independent Television has been a national institution, in fact as well as in name, for the last quarter century. To suggest that it should be renamed the Regional Television Authority, as was put forward in one of Annan's more half-hearted recommendations,[20] was not only belittling but a misnomer. Fortunately it found few, if any, friends and was in due course rejected in the Labour Government's White Paper which was published in July 1978.[21]

Regional programming, in the sense of programmes intended to be of particular interest to viewers resident in the area covered by an ITV company, are and always have been an element in Independent Television. Each company covers local events and personalities on a daily basis, and regards this as a specific and vital part of its responsibilities. All the time efforts are being made to improve the quality of the coverage and standards have risen steadily over the years. The fact remains that programming of this sort is of its nature regional. It cannot be local in the way that local radio can, nor can it hope to rival local newspapers in the intensive coverage given to a restricted area. The television signal broadcast from the present UHF transmitters can be received by large numbers of people, often counted in millions, in the main areas of population. Its unique characteristic is its efficiency and economy in permitting communication to be made with so many people at the same time. Of course not all of them are interested in the same things. Hence the art and skill, indeed the very name, of the broadcaster.

Nor can regional programming be converted by a stroke of the pen into network programming for national audiences. Occasionally, programmes produced for regional viewing in one part of the country may serve the needs of a wider national audience, but that is or should be a coincidence. Regional programmes are the provincial journalism of television, an essential part of a free society and demanding of great integrity and professionalism in their production. The network programmes, originating not just in London but in certain other major centres of population, are national in the same way as Fleet Street newspapers and national magazines and periodicals are national. The aims and the approach are quite distinct.

V

Both of these strands of programming come together in the service which each of the fifteen ITV companies provides for viewers in its own region. The component parts: network programmes, regional programmes, national and international news from ITN, acquired feature films or filmed series, are then scheduled in a sequence and at times that are calculated to appeal to the viewing audience. The great majority of this audience over the country as a whole now has the capacity of receiving two BBC television channels, BBC 1 and BBC 2, as well as ITV. The drawing up of a programme schedule is a

skilled process involving much detailed planning. The two BBC
controllers in charge of scheduling BBC 1 and BBC 2 have an
advantage in that they can act more quickly and independently
than their colleagues in ITV who need to agree among themselves before implementing any major decision effecting the
network programmes shown on the single ITV channel.

With two channels at its disposal the BBC can provide what
is in effect a unified and comprehensive television service. The
programmes are produced by specialist groups and offered to
the Controller of one or other channel. Each of the two Controllers has a considerable measure of autonomy, but they will
liaise closely. Thus a drama series, or an entertainment programme, for example, can be tried out on one channel and if
successful then repeated on the other. Long sports events, such
as tennis and golf, can be covered on one channel, probably
during the afternoon, continuing on the other in the evening,
with the interested audience switching channels without any
inconvenience or interruption. The BBC aims to make the
scheduling of programmes on its two channels complementary.
This does not mean, as is sometime thought, that there is
necessarily a straight choice offered between a serious item on
the one channel and a light one on the other. The aim is rather
to provide the viewer with a reasonable choice for as much of
the time as possible. As the BBC pointed out in evidence to the
Annan Committee it is not possible to divide up the full range
of programmes shown on its two channels into perfectly balanced
alternatives in terms of programme categories. Some alternatives cause as much frustration as they do pleasure:

> *Sportsnight* on BBC 1 opposite *Elizabeth R* on BBC 2 was a
> case in point. It did not simply provide the burden of choice;
> it divided households. It had to be changed: and was
> changed quickly.[22]

Complementary programme planning is facilitated by syn-
chronizing the start-times of as many BBC programmes as
possible in the course of an evening so that the viewer may
choose what he wishes to see at these common programme
junctions. This is current BBC practice, but it is something

which is denied to ITV until there is a second ITV channel planned in conjunction with the first.

As things have worked out over recent years the national television audience divides more or less equally in the viewing of BBC and ITV. In the early years ITV built up a large lead, but the BBC responded with a more popular approach to programming on BBC 1, supplemented since 1964 by BBC 2. This fifty-fifty division is far from static. It varies from week to week and season to season. Nor does it result from any sort of inbuilt balance between the two services. On the contrary, BBC 1 and ITV schedules are planned in keen competition with each other with the aim of maximizing to the full extent the audience for a particular type of programme. Important though ratings are as an indication of audience response, in neither service are they permitted to override all other considerations. In ITV many well-established programmes are regularly transmitted over the network which are accepted as being unlikely to achieve the same size of audience as entertainment programming. These include *World in Action, TV Eye, Weekend World*, certain documentaries, some plays, opera and ballet, as well as educational and religious programmes which are subject to special provisions. Each of these is recognized as a worthwhile element contributing to a schedule of programmes intended to appeal to a wide range of audience interests.

Should the lure of the ratings prove too great a temptation in ITV, likely to occur more as a result of a bout of over-competitiveness caused by a successful run on BBC 1 than from any pressure on the part of advertisers, the IBA stands as a guardian of what it interprets as being in the best interests of the viewing public. The Authority's approach, both on matters effecting the composition of the schedule and on the content of individual programmes, may and at times does differ from that of the companies. Despite occasional friction on the surface, the underlying relationship between the regulatory body, established by statute, which does not itself produce programmes, and the companies which it licences to do so, has been a vital and healthy one. The IBA has the last word, as is right and proper, and the companies accept this even though some producers seek to challenge it periodically. At the same time the Authority acknowledges that programmes cannot be made by edict or bureaucratic intervention. They result from a complex creative process which is located squarely within the programme companies. In truth this is their *raison d'être*.

After a lengthy and exhaustive enquiry, lasting two-and-a-half years and costing £315,000, the report of the Annan Committee concluded that 'competition between the BBC and Independent Television had raised the standard of programmes under both Authorities',[23] and indeed common observation by anyone who has viewed television regularly over the last twenty-five years would bear this out. The Report commented that not only had competition helped to act as a spur to the production of good programmes, but it had led to greater account being taken of popular demand as well as providing workers in the industry with some choice of employment. Annan stressed that competition should always be for variety and excellence and not just for audiences. Few broadcasters would disagree.

Apart from those who wish to restructure broadcasting for ideological reasons, competition between BBC and ITV has been generally accepted as beneficial. As already explained it is regulated, not unrestricted competition, since the members of the IBA and BBC Board of Governors can bring their influence to bear to ensure that the zeal of the professional broadcasters does not get out of hand. The problem of schedule clashes, however, continues to irritate the public and to be the source of a considerable volume of complaint from viewers. To some extent it is inevitable. As Lord Hill remarked in evidence to the Annan Committee: 'Occasional clashes are a small price to pay for the stimulus of competition.'[23] One such clash is to be found in *World in Action*, Granada's regular current affairs programme for ITV, which is scheduled on Monday evenings, usually overlapping with *Panorama* on BBC 1. Annan referred to this example, but replied robustly:

. . . when Sweden decided to eliminate such clashes and transmitted light entertainment at the same time as a current affairs programme, the flight of the audience from current affairs was such as to make the authorities fear for the ideal of an educated democracy. Competition between the Broadcasting Authorities cannot be eliminated. It is not merely advertisers but the broadcasters themselves, the men and women who make the programmes, who want large audiences and a peak time showing for their programmes.[23]

VI

As relations between the BBC and Independent Television have improved over the years most of the old animosity has worn off. Dyed-in-the-wool BBC characters who found it hard to accept or treat with those who had undermined their privileged position gave way to a newer breed of executives. Some of these have worked on both sides of the broadcasting fence and in fact the present director-general of the BBC, the managing-director, BBC Television, and the controller of BBC 2 have all worked in ITV in the past. Similarly several senior executives in Independent Television, including the managing-directors of three out of the five central companies and the director of television at the IBA, have worked for the BBC. There is consequently a closeness of professional contact which usually allows sensible decisions to be reached when the interests of both broadcasting organizations are involved. For example national occasions can sometimes be televised only on the basis of one set of cameras rather than two, and vision and sound links are also sometimes shared. Television coverage of the Royal Variety performance is alternated annually. There is a friendly liaison on matters effecting British broadcasting which arise at the European Broadcasting Union and other international bodies. When rival claims as to audience size were criticized by Annan, even though they resulted from different methods of gathering data, it was agreed without too much difficulty to set up a joint audience research system. This aims to make possible the assembly of research data drawn from a common source which will be available to both broadcasting organizations, as well as to other users.

The only real exception to these commonsense approaches to matters of potential conflict has been in the coverage of sport. For many years BBC and ITV have each covered a range of sporting events. The BBC, with the advantage of two channels for scheduling, has given it a higher priority and has built up a large and highly-skilled sports group. ITV has concentrated particularly on horse racing and football, although the range has widened considerably in recent years. Few except the most fanatic supporters of a particular sport can now claim that there is much to choose between ITV's *World of Sport* and the BBC's *Grandstand* on Saturday afternoons.

It is, however, the sport which is transmitted in the evening which is the primary cause of schedule clashes. This is never more conspicuous or leads to more outcry than over major international sporting events in the calendar, notably the World Cup Football series. In 1978 World Cup Football matches from Argentina were covered for some seventy hours each on BBC 1 and ITV over a period of two weeks. For nine of these hours the picture was identical on both channels at the same time. Much of the remainder was simultaneous coverage of different matches and discussion and analysis by different panels of experts. But to the non-sporting audience, football is football. This sort of scheduling, which seems to put the competitive interests of the broadcasting organization above its responsibility to the audience as a whole, appears incomprehensible to the viewer, and has been the subject of much complaint and argument. It was remarked upon in the White Paper on Broadcasting published in 1978. While declining to intervene the Government acknowledged that:

> . . . many people are irritated when both broadcasting authorities broadcast the same event at the same time (particularly when it is a sporting event or series of events and both authorities broadcast the same picture) and hopes that the Authorities . . . will find ways of keeping these instances to a minimum. This is a matter on which the public has a right to expect them to reach a sensible agreement between themselves.[24]

Even this official nudge towards sanity was not enough to produce results. The broadcasting organizations discussed the problem separately, but failed to agree. The next step was a vigorous exchange of letters between the chairman of the BBC, Sir Michael Swann, and the chairman of the IBA, Lady Plowden – the 'Dear Michael/Dear Bridget' correspondence as it became known when published in the press. The IBA reiterated its contention, strongly supported by the ITV companies, that television coverage of major sporting events should be alternated between BBC and ITV. There were various ways of accomplishing this, but in each case the objective was the same; namely to ensure that the viewer did not receive duplicate coverage of the same event. The BBC reply claimed a pre-eminence in sports coverage which it felt could not be surrendered to its competitor. In his letter to Lady Plowden dated 6 October 1978 Sir Michael Swann asserted that there was a clear disparity between the BBC's commitment to sport of all kinds and that of the ITV companies. He went on to say that the BBC governors had asked themselves this question:

Does the Authority believe that, in view of the ITV Companies' record in sports of all kinds over the past 25 years, it should succeed by political pressure in forcing the BBC to withdraw from three weeks' coverage of the Olympic Games or the two weeks of the World Cup? The answer is obvious and we cannot see how we could ever accept it.

There may have been some justification for this argument in regard to the Olympic Games, since it was true that the BBC provided a wider, all-the-year-round, coverage than ITV of athletics, as well as of equestrian and swimming events, between Olympics. Indeed ITV, after much argument and with considerable reluctance, had stood down from comprehensive coverage of the 1976 Munich Olympics, partly on these grounds, in order to avoid duplication. For football there was none. A limited form of alternation had been negotiated for the coverage of the World Cup matches in 1978, although in the event it proved unsatisfactory, resulting in around seventy hours of football being shown on each majority channel, most of it in peak time, most of it simultaneous. This served to focus public attention once more on the lack of choice caused by the overwhelming concentration on football, with large sums of money involved for fees and to meet the accompanying facility and transmission charges. It was an unfortunate situation and one which left large sections of the audience bemused and resentful.

The deadlock only began to break late in 1978 when London Weekend Television, acting on behalf of the ITV Network, negotiated an exclusive contract with the Football League for the television coverage of all of its matches for three years from 1979 onwards. This would have effectively knocked out the popular Saturday night *Match of the Day* from the BBC schedules and left it in a much weaker competitive position in the coverage of football. The speed and unexpectedness of the coup caught the BBC on the hop. Now it was the Corporation rather than the public which was bemused and resentful. The BBC complained strenuously that it had come to expect joint negotiation with the Football League and that it regarded uni-lateral action as a breach of faith, if not of the law. Legal actions were initiated to obtain an injunction and to test the position in the Courts. Commenting on behalf of the ITV companies, Bryan Cowgill, chairman of the Network Sports Committee and formerly a senior BBC executive, put the position con-cisely:

It has occurred to many of us in ITV that this is the only answer to the BBC's continued intransigence about alterna-tion, when they have refused reasonable requests from ITV to alternate, for example, the Olympic Games and the World Cup. This intransigence is annoying the public. Failing agreements to end duplication the answer will increasingly lie in exclusivity.

As so often happens, power provided a leverage where reason and persuasion had failed. In the Spring of 1979 the BBC with-drew its High Court action, and agreed to share with In-dependent Television coverage of week-end Football League matches throughout the season on a rotating basis. For the first year of a four-year contract the BBC would provide recorded coverage of League matches on Saturday evenings, while ITV would show recorded matches on Sunday afternoons. In the following year the position would be reversed, with the pattern of alternation repeating itself in the third and fourth years.

Associated with this agreement was a fresh and constructive attempt to break the impasse over the Olympics in 1980 and the

World Cup in 1982. This resulted in an agreement being reached that during the 1982 World Football Cup in Spain there would be no simultaneous coverage of matches other than the final on BBC 1 and ITV, although special arrangements would have to be made if two teams from the United Kingdom (for example England and Scotland) happened to be playing at the same time. It was also agreed to treat the two weeks of the 1980 European Football Championships in the same manner, with no simultaneous transmission of any matches other than the Final, except in the case of two UK teams playing at the same time.

For the Olympic Games due to take place in Moscow in the Summer of 1980, it was agreed to avoid duplication during the peak viewing hours of 8.00 p.m.–10.30 p.m. in the evenings. Before the participation by Western athletes was thrown into doubt by the Russian aggression in Afghanistan, the BBC and ITV had intended to provide a full coverage of the games, both by way of live transmissions by satellite and recorded highlights, but to schedule the coverage in such a way as to avoid simultaneous transmissions in peak time.

These agreements, notified to the Office of Fair Trading, represented a break-through: a willingness by both broadcasting organizations to work towards the avoidance of simultaneous transmission of events taking place outside the United Kingdom, particularly when the picture source is common to both. It is, however, unlikely to be the end of the story. There will be other events, less conspicuous than the Olympics and World Cup, and other rivalries. Professionalism among the programme makers, the subject of the next chapter, and a fierce sense of competitiveness run strongly among those working on sports journalism in BBC and ITV. It is both understandable and creditable that they should be so motivated, but it would not be right that they should have the last word. Priority should always be given to orientating the programmes towards the needs of the audience before satisfying the zeal of the programme makers. If the person to whom a message is addressed is not willing to listen, then no communication can take place.

All in all the episode was a particularly illuminating one. It shows that even those responsible for the conduct of a great public corporation, in this case the governors of the BBC, with their loyalties divided between their desire to uphold the interests and morale of their staff and their duty to the public, are sometimes capable in all good faith of putting the cart before the horse.

4

Television:
The Programme Makers

I

One of the consequences of the periodic public reviews of broadcasting referred to in the previous chapters is that informed debate on broadcasting issues tends to concentrate attention on proposals for changing various aspects of organization. After the generalities are got out of the way the practical and tidy British mind, particularly if Whitehall officials are involved, turns towards ideas for new authorities; such as an Open Broadcasting Authority; a Local Broadcasting Authority; a Public Enquiry Board for Broadcasting; or service management Boards for the BBC. All of these suggestions were put forward either by the Annan Committee or by the Labour Government in the five-year period of review which lasted from 1974 to 1979. None in the event came to fruition, but each provoked much argument. This emphasis on the structure and forms of broadcasting, so enticing to administrators and social reformers, can become narrow and artificial if it is not taken together with a broader consideration of the way in which programmes, good or bad, get made and of the factors which determine their production.

The values which infuse broadcasting are largely the values of the programme makers, influenced and guided as they are by programme managements and the regulatory authorities. It is on these values far more than on factors connected with structure and organization that the standards of British broadcasting ultimately depend. Of course it is true that the two always interrelate, but much of the public discussion gives inadequate attention to the role of the programme maker in the broadcast environment. It is also true that many of the spokesmen for broadcast interests who have participated in the policy debates in the wake of the three major post-war reviews – Beveridge which reported in 1951, Pilkington in the early sixties, and Annan in the late seventies – have got drawn into arguing the pros and cons of organizational change.

Successive BBC managements have resisted proposals for splitting up the BBC into separate corporations for television, radio and the external services, and have fought against the idea of superimposing upon each service a management board including a proportion of direct Ministerial appointees. Executives from the ITV companies and spokesmen for the Independent Broadcasting Authority have similarly argued their corner for a second channel for ITV. Independent producers favoured an Open Broadcasting Authority, separate from the existing authorities and acting more in the manner of a publishing house as a means of getting more of their work on the air; while some of the advertisers preferred a fourth channel in direct competition with the existing ITV contractors in order to move towards a more price competitive market for advertising their products.

The idea of an Open Broadcasting Authority, advocated by Annan as a move away from the duopoly exercised by BBC and ITV, was only adopted by the Labour Government after some division within its Parliamentary Party and Ministerial ranks, and without any great display of enthusiasm. The Conservative Party in Opposition had committed itself to allocating the vacant fourth channel to the IBA and lost no time in declaring its aims after the General Election which took place in May 1979. In the Queen's Speech on 15 May the incoming government stated:

> Proposals will be brought before you for the future of broadcasting. A Bill will be introduced to extend the life of the Independent Broadcasting Authority, which will be given responsibility – subject to strict safeguards – for the Fourth Television channel.[1]

As Home Secretary, William Whitelaw assumed responsibility for government policy towards broadcasting matters. He was no novice, having previously had intimate contact, both as Chief Whip and as Lord President of the Council, with virtually all of the issues and controversies which had arisen between broadcasters and the politicians throughout the decade. In Northern Ireland too he had to deal with reporters and the broadcasting authorities on various highly-charged occasions. Remarkably for a man who held the office of Secretary of State for Northern Ireland (the first to do so) at the height of the crisis in 1972–3, Whitelaw's own relations with television and radio were close and friendly, avoiding disputes like the row over *A Question of Ulster* before direct rule and some of the angry incidents that were to erupt later during the tenure of his successors. At the Royal Television Society's Convention at Cambridge in September 1979 he affirmed his own commitment. Broadcasting and its relationship to a free society, he observed at the start of his speech, 'was a subject in which I have been personally interested, and involved from a political point of view, over many years'.

After describing in some detail the government's approach to the utilization of the fourth channel and the principles on which it should be based, Whitelaw ended by reiterating that the broadcasters should be independent of government in the day-to-day conduct of their business:

. . . the broadcasting authorities should continue to be responsible for the content of programmes, for ensuring that the services are conducted in the general public interest and are in accordance with the requirements and objectives which Parliament places on each authority. In all I have said today, I want to underline the Government's determination to adhere to this system. As the Annan Committee commented, the authorities are themselves accountable to Parliament for their decisions, and the services they provide, and Parliament itself is accountable to the electorate. This is the system we must maintain as a basis for television in a free society here in the United Kingdom.[2]

The new Home Secretary was personally popular and on good terms with a large number of the more influential people on both sides of the divide which separates broadcasting from party politics. To the politicians he carried weight, while to the broadcasters his heart was evidently in the right place. Thus he enjoyed support to an unusual degree amongst both groups. Why, then, with such a powerful Minister, with a grasp of the subject, combining both popularity and shrewdness, did the proposal run into such heavy weather? In his Cambridge speech Whitelaw had prescribed that the fourth channel should offer a distinctive service of its own, appealing to tastes and interests not adequately provided for on the existing channels. At least initially it would take the form of a single national service without regional variations. A proportion of the programmes would be supplied by the major ITV network companies operating in the central areas under the arrangements described in the last chapter. But they would not be allowed to dominate (this was one of the more explicit of the 'strict safeguards' referred to in the Queen's Speech), and both the regional companies and independent producers outside the present ITV system altogether would be encouraged to contribute. News would be supplied by ITN, and educational interests would also have access to the new channel.

It all sounded encouraging enough and within two months the IBA published a detailed blueprint of how it might work in practice. The device of a secondary board or trust to which the fourth channel would be answerable was put forward. The IBA saw this as a way of distancing both the programme companies – strict safeguards again – and to a certain extent the Authority itself from the management of the service. The Board of the Channel Four company, with an outside chairman and deputy-chairman, would be drawn from those interests likely to be supplying the programmes. The ITV companies which, in addition to providing an unspecified proportion of the programmes, would be providing all of the finance, might be represented by four directors, with five more directors able to speak on behalf of other potential suppliers of programmes, including independent producers and film makers as well as educational bodies. The ITV representatives would thus be in a minority. The Board would appoint its own chief executive and/or a programme controller. The Authority, while maintaining ultimate control, would not be directly represented.

As regards its mode of operation, it was envisaged that the Fourth Channel company would not produce its own programmes, but would commission and acquire them from others. Having done so it would schedule them on ITV 2 in a way that was complementary, rather than competitive, with the service at present provided on ITV. As charged by the Home Secretary the service would aim to have a distinctive character, probably appealing to audiences considerably smaller than those viewing on the present majority channels. Indeed in its published plan the IBA spoke of 'a service visited from time to time rather than watched constantly, as BBC 1 and ITV 1 have tended to be by significant parts of their audience'.[3] The same controls on content, such as the family viewing policy restricting scenes of violence or other material unsuitable for children until after 9.00 p.m., would apply and the finance – estimated at some £70–80 million annually – would be provided by the ITV companies by way of subscriptions paid out of revenues obtained from the sale of advertisements on ITV 1 and ITV 2 in their own franchise areas.

The plan was reasonable and carefully thought out. It certainly followed from much discussion and putting forward of views. But in attempting to placate too many conflicting interests it ended up by pleasing none. Essentially it was conceived as a compromise between an Open Broadcasting Authority and a straightforward extension of the present system, for instance by the appointment of additional programme companies, wholly separate as to finance and control, in each franchise area. In Parliament it is probable that a majority of members of the Labour Party would have preferred the former; a majority of Conservatives the latter. What emerged was a hybrid solution satisfactory neither to the independent producers and film makers of the Channel Four Group, led by Richard Hoggart and Phillip Whitehead, MP, nor to the advertisers and free-traders who wanted more direct competition. This body of opinion supported by the Confederation of British Industry and the Incorporated Society of British Advertisers was opposed to what they saw as a perpetuation, indeed an extension, of the monopoly enjoyed in the sale of advertisement time in each region by the ITV companies. Then it was reported in the press in January 1980[4] that the Prime Minister was unhappy that the scheme would result in a loss to the Treasury of a substantial part of the proceeds of the additional payments made by the ITV companies to the Exchequer by way of a special levy on their profits. This amounts to two-thirds of pre-tax profits, after allowing for an initial tax-free slice. In the financial year 1978–9 the levy brought in some £69 millions, and it is on the existence of this cushion that the financial viability of ITV 2 will depend, at any rate for the first few years after its launch.

It should be emphasized that the arguments in favour of the proposal evolved by the IBA and the Home Office are also strong. Annan and both governments which considered his report concluded that competitive advertising on the two ITV channels would inevitably result in a move towards maximizing the audiences for the programmes. This would in its turn effect the programming on ITV 1, with the strong possibility of spilling over in due course to the BBC. The tradition of complementary programming and regulated competition runs deep. But so do the political opinions of those who will decide the issue in Parliament, few of whom are closely involved with the intricacies of broadcasting policy.

No one can be sure of the outcome, although when it finally arrives, the fourth television channel will in all probability be the last extension of broadcasting to be established within the institutionalized framework that we have become familiar with over the years since the birth of broadcasting in the twenties. I return to a view of the future in the final chapter.

II

Whatever else may be said about the tortuous way in which public policy has emerged as regards the use made of the fourth channel, no one can deny that the programme makers have had a conspicuous and influential voice. It has not always been so. In fact so much of the debate on broadcasting matters usually revolves around questions of organizational structure and control that the craft considerations, out of which have sprung many of the finest achievements of British television, are too often obscured. One notable figure who has consistently claimed that it is primarily the way the programmes get made that matters above all else is Sir Denis Forman. Now chairman of Granada Television, and with a lifetime's experience of working in films and television, Forman has played as large a part as anyone still active in broadcasting in influencing and guiding collective opinion within Independent Television and setting standards. Sir Huw Wheldon did something of the same at the BBC. In the Fleming Memorial Lecture delivered to the Royal Television Society in 1973 Forman described in a memorable phrase the making of programmes as 'the most mysterious and by far the most important part of the television organism'. His argument was that it is the contribution of the programme makers that is absolutely essential to British television. Those set in authority over the programme makers, he concluded:

> should always remember that alongside allotting fre-
> quencies and parcelling out the land in regions and broad-
> casting stations, their chief raison d'être is to create the
> right climate for the programme makers. Control and
> censorship are, of course, a part of their duties, but the
> smaller the part can naturally become, the less importance
> it can assume, the better.[5]

This aspect of television – the craft of programme making and the conditions in which it is most likely to flourish – is largely unknown to the public, yet it is of great significance. Broadcast programmes whether on radio or television are brought into existence as a result of an organic process of individuals or creative groups working together. Many are freelancers: most of the writers; some of the producers and directors; virtually all of the actors, the entertainers and the musicians. The remainder are employed on contract or are members of the permanent staff. The talents and latent crea-tivity of all have to be nurtured and developed. Programme makers and programme managements have to coexist side by side; the work of one cannot reach the screen without the consent of the other. This is the prime function of the broad-casting organization, whatever shape it may take, however it is financed, and however it is held accountable to the public it serves.

It follows therefore that the structure of the broadcasting organization should be secondary to the programmes. Although this order of priorities may seem self-evident when baldly stated, it is not in fact widely accepted in official circles. Nevertheless it is the case that novelty and originality only come to full flower when gifted programme makers coalesce in an atmosphere of mutual confidence with competent and experienced programme managements. The contribution made by programme managements to this partnership should not be underestimated. Every so often a group of highly regarded programme makers combine in a joint undertaking with a common purpose. The initial London Weekend consortium which won a franchise from the IBA in 1967 and, earlier, Television Reporters International were examples. Both failed, not because of any sudden loss of skill or inventiveness by the programme makers, but because they were not held together by sufficiently strong managements.

Stable sources of finance are also necessary for solid foundations. There are no formulae which prescribe success and no short cuts. Blueprints of organization cannot produce good television: they have to be interpreted, moulded and adapted to fit the people they circumscribe. The audience too responds and makes itself felt. Such influences extend beyond representations made by politicians, departments of central and local government, and special interest groups. They include the published opinions of professional television critics; continuous and systematic research on what is known of the size of audiences and the reaction to and enjoyment of programmes; and comments received from community groups or private individuals by direct contact. What results is a creative organization, dynamic, often in a state of tension, but always containing the key to the qualitative achievement of good television.

Within this environment certain fixed factors and practices will have a conditioning effect on the atmosphere in which programmes get made. Budgets, the availability of production facilities, time, restrictions of one kind or another on content: all are unavoidable and all have an impact. More elusive are the values and standards held by people working in television.

(Contrary to popular belief it is only a small minority, mainly of writers and producers, who have a burning conviction about a particular message they wish to communicate. The majority look on their work as an end in itself rather than as a means to an end. At a production centre the general impression given is of a group of people carrying out with varying degrees of enthusiasm professional or technical tasks which only incidentally involve the communication of messages.)

(The climate of opinion within a studio or production centre is pervasive and varies somewhat between one establishment and another. This is important in that a house style will have an effect on such topical issues as the extent to which violent action on the screen is justified; the language that is used, especially in scripted programmes; and the approach to what is regarded as the balanced reporting of politics. Although guidelines exist they are not immutable, and there is plenty of room for differences of opinion over what is, or is not, acceptable.)

III

The producer is at the centre of the process from which television programmes result; but he does not stand alone. He is surrounded by a creative team of director, writer, designer, researcher and other specialists and is answerable to a programme management. In the BBC and most of the ITV companies producers work direct to programme department heads, who in their turn are responsible to a Programme Controller. The Controller reports to a chief executive, and to a board of directors or a board of management. Brooding over the whole output of the service is one or other of the statutory broadcasting authorities – the laymen acting for a term as governors of the BBC or members of the IBA – who maintain regular contact within the programme managements and whose functions are described in Chapter 2.

At each level of decision-taking public opinion makes itself felt, both as an expression of general values and in terms of specific objects being pursued by active pressure groups. This applies in BBC Television and ITV alike, as it does in local and network radio, and as it would in any alternative that was likely to be set up in place of the existing system.

The role of the programme maker in the BBC has been investigated in great detail by Tom Burns. In his book *The BBC – Public Institution and Private World*,[6] which should be required reading for anyone interested in the way in which a creative organization functions, Professor Burns summarizes the findings of two sets of interviews carried out with BBC staff in 1963 and again in 1973. He describes the BBC as a working community and occupational milieu, and records the shift that has taken place away from the Reithian concept of public service towards the new god of professionalism. To get the flavour of the prevailing orthodoxy of the BBC in the decade between 1945–55, however, it is necessary to go back earlier than the period covered by these interviews.

One of the most determined and clear-minded broadcasters of the immediate post-war era was Grace Wyndham Goldie. She has recalled:

> . . . we had the confidence, the faith, the optimism and, no doubt, the arrogance, of that distant generation. Standards of integrity and quality in broadcast communication had been established in sound radio as a result of the work of the institution of which we were members, the British Broadcasting Corporation. This fact had earned it the respect and admiration of the world. However passionately we might challenge some of the judgements made within the Corporation we believed, equally passionately, in its basic aims. It was our task to see that these were translated into action in terms of visual language of the newer medium of television.[7]

It must be questionable whether the public service idealism of the Corporation and its staff would have survived into the sixties, even in conditions of continued monopoly. The BBC would not have been able to stand apart from the rest of the public service, including the central core of the Civil Service itself, which witnessed a gradual erosion of the traditional ideals. The causes lay deep in the roots of the social changes that were coming to the surface after two decades of peace. In broadcasting there can be little doubt that the demise of the Reithian approach was hastened by the advent of Independent Television in 1955. Although it can be argued convincingly that the newcomer, regulated and supervised as it was by a specially appointed public authority, was also operating as a form of public service broadcasting, this was not evident to the public at large; still less to the employees of the BBC.

ITV simply did not represent what had come to be understood by the term 'public service broadcasting'. The overtones of high-mindedness and self-improvement were noticeably absent. In their place was an emphasis on entertainment and informality. Moreover, the new type of programmes rapidly established themselves as exceedingly popular with the viewing audience, until before long 70 per cent of those with sets capable of receiving both channels had indicated a clear preference for ITV. In the early sixties the BBC under Hugh Greene, the first director-general to be appointed from within the BBC, fought back vigorously. As one of his ITV competitors was aptly to remark, 'When Sir Hugh Greene issued the order of the day that the BBC should get 50 per cent of the audience, the Corporation responded with almost indecent relish.'[8] The result was an insistence that BBC programmes should be entertaining; that they should appeal to the audience; and that they should compete effectively with the programmes being shown at the same time as the rival channel.

The increasing emphasis on entertainment did not mean that the BBC jettisoned its traditional output in the fields of documentary, drama, music, religious and educational programmes. On the contrary such programmes survived and prospered, although changed in content and approach, and as such appealed to larger numbers of people than ever before. While the BBC learned much about entertainment from the commercial companies in the early years, so ITV benefited from the BBC's high standards in factual programming. If ITN broke fresh ground in the presentation of news, as it did, the BBC was to pioneer developments in the coverage of sport. As such the two services grew closer together in their output, each gaining from the strengths of the other. The public responded positively to the new style of television that was emerging, and the audience grew both in size and discrimination. Before long it became clear that the total viewing audience was dividing fairly evenly on a fifty-fifty basis between BBC and ITV, and this is a pattern that has endured generally ever since. So it was that a new and genuinely democratic imperative became established: henceforth television in Britain should be a popular service.

If the competitiveness of ITV programming, and the consequent impact on the viewers in the fifties was to be the primary cause of the radical change in attitudes within the BBC, other factors were also at work. Between 1954–6 the four original ITV companies: Associated-Rediffusion, ATV, ABC Television and Granada had to establish themselves in a very short period of time. The only available qualified staff with broadcasting experience were either employed by the BBC, or were ex-BBC, or were working abroad, particularly in Canada. Large numbers of staff, many of them enterprising younger employees, left the BBC to join ITV. Most received the offer of higher salaries as an inducement, but the opportunities of being in at the start of a new enterprise and the promise of a freer and less stuffy creative environment also played an important part. Their departure disrupted the BBC and undermined still further the already shaky idealism of the public service.

Much of the thrust and brashness of the new television service came from this group of people. They were determined to make the most of the opportunities offered and to demonstrate they could produce programmes of quality and spirit in a setting quite different to that of the BBC. Yet to what body of principle could the inner man working in broadcasting, irrespective of channel, turn for solace or for justification of his actions? There is a need for such points of reference in most forms of human activity. It is as if deep down men and women require a reassurance that what they are doing in their working lives is worthwhile, not merely in providing means of subsistence, but in some wider scheme of things. Motivation, whether of people in groups or singly, is always complex and it is never wise to generalize too dogmatically about what moves human beings to behave in the way they do. In broadcasting, as in other occupations, motives differ widely. Nevertheless it can be noted as a milestone in the history of broadcasting that as public service idealism went into decline, the concept which came increasingly to replace it amongst programme makers was the idea of professionalism.

IV

It was in the BBC of the sixties that a new frame of reference was most urgently needed and it was within the BBC that the seeds of professionalism as an alternative creed first germinated. Professionalism in broadcasting had in fact existed and been admired inside and outside the BBC for many years in the sense of a competent, qualified approach to the craft of programme production. The term 'professionalism' really stood for little more than the mastery of a body of knowledge and was contrasted with amateurishness. The standards it implied were less precise, and generally a great deal less demanding, than those required by professions with a membership limited by examination or other qualification, such as medicine or the law, architecture or engineering. Nor was there any code of conduct enforced by a professional body with disciplinary power. Despite these shortcomings, the trend towards a looser professionalism was not peculiar to broadcasting, practice, although it flourished mightily in the hothouse. According to Tom Burns:

> The word 'professionalism' had, by 1963, an extraordinarily wide currency throughout the BBC. There were times when it seemed that the word was being credited among programme staff with an almost talismanic quality, representing some absolute principle by which to judge people and achievement. Ten years later the word seem to occur even more frequently, to have acquired a wider and more potent range of meanings and connotations, and to be used throughout all reaches of the corporation.[9]

The same trend was evident across the Atlantic. In 1967 Fred W. Friendly, formerly President of CBS News who had resigned following an argument over news coverage, dedicated his informative and witty book, *Due To Circumstances Beyond Our Control*,[10] 'For the professionals at CBS News'.

What had first been added by usage to the basic idea of best practice was the perspective of freshness and originality. A programme maker was regarded as professional not just because he was proficient at his job, but because he was admired by his fellows for qualities which he brought to it which were out of the ordinary. The next layer of meaning to be superimposed was that of dedication or commitment. Here again the organic change that was taking place inside the private world of the BBC was mirroring stormy waters outside. The sixties were a period of dissent, of decolonization, of violent revolutionary change showing itself even in such deeply rooted societies as the French Republic. Commitment to one's own values stood higher than the acceptance of those embraced collectively by others and enshrined in the form of established institutions.

Within broadcasting, commitment ran in parallel with a questioning and scrutiny of authority: a feature of the old public service idealism which no doubt made the irreverence and iconoclasm of the early *Tonight* programme and its successors rather more acceptable to the Board of Governors and senior management of the BBC than might otherwise have been the case. Some of the most notable programmes were produced by young men such as Donald Baverstock, Michael Peacock and Antony Jay. None of them had any background in journalism, although the function of most of the programmes which they produced was mainly journalistic. Once established in current affairs and documentary programmes, the idea of commitment quickly spread to drama where it survives to this day.

Through an accretion of meanings the word 'professionalism' thus came to stand for much more than the competent performance of a task. In the BBC, and then in ITV too when once the first flush of enthusiasm had worn off and the need for a frame of reference manifested itself, the regard of fellow programme makers for the way in which a programme fulfilled its aims became a dominating concern. Whether or not it became *the* dominating concern is open to debate. But it was undoubtedly a common strand, and there can be little argument that the notion of true professionalism, and the respect engendered by this concept, did much to influence or condition the prevailing ethos, to some extent filling the void left by the decline of the public service ideal.

While it would be misleading to rest too confidently on the theory that professionalism displaced entirely public service idealism as a motivating force in broadcasting, just as it is unwise to depend too much on any theory which seeks to explain all the infinite mysteries of human conduct, this approach nevertheless throws some light on the inner workings of the television organism. It is difficult, if not impossible, to say with any certainty what is uppermost in the mind of the programme maker as he goes about his task. Motives will vary and any generalization needs to be treated with caution. The preoccupations of an editor working on a daily news programme are unlikely to correspond with those of a drama producer. But a keen concern with the quality of performance, as it is assessed and appraised by persons regarded as fellow professionals inside and outside the broadcasting organization, is common to producers and directors, writers and artists, managers and technicians. In this sense particularly, professionalism has come to take the place of the outwardly directed concern with the use of broadcasting for the betterment of the public which was inherent in Mrs Wyndham Goldie's recollection. Insofar as any common ethos exists today within the BBC and Independent Broadcasting it is loosely centred around factors of this sort.

The current of professionalism runs strongest among those who are most closely involved with the production of programmes. Others within the broadcasting organization are occupied in providing support services, or in scheduling programmes for transmission, or in ensuring that the broadcast signals are efficiently transmitted for the best possible reception in the home. In all of this commitment and dedication have a part. But controllers and boards of directors, while sharing and contributing to this ethos, also have to be mindful of a set of wider considerations, concerned more with the relationship between the programme and its audience, rather than with the intentions of the producer. This raises the fundamental dilemma in broadcasting which is how to reconcile the exercise of authority in the public interest with the freedom necessary to the creative process.

Justifications for controls on the programme maker include the need to observe certain principles of accuracy and fairness in the reporting of events. Then there are standards of what is expected as regards matters of taste in entertainment programmes; and the perennial problems, in drama especially, arising out of the portrayal of violence, the showing of explicit sexual scenes and the use of bad language. Each of these has to be balanced with the legitimate desire of the programme maker to express what he wants to say in his own way.

The first standard that the public is entitled to expect is that what is broadcast in factual programmes is true and accurate. In Britain and the United States, as in many other parts of the world, this maxim has been accepted without question. There may be and often are arguments about what constitutes the truth, for example in the reporting of industrial disputes.[11] What appears to one viewer to be a fair conclusion arising out of comments made by the spokesman for the employers or the union representatives may seem to another to reveal a conspicuous bias. Sometimes, too, there are difficult judgements to be made regarding the recognition of interests or interest groups for the purposes of enabling its spokesman to communicate with the public by means of the broadcast media. Professionalism in the news room, where items are selected and edited, and professional conduct by reporters and commentators, have helped to entrench practices based on an ideal of fairness which underpins the search for truth. Only a full picture will normally contribute to a true picture, and certain assumptions need to be made in the selection of information. The highest aims may not always be achieved in the heat of the moment, but the fact that such aims prevail, and in the main resist challenge, is a fundamental and encouraging mark of a free society. So is the existence of machinery, in the form of the regulatory authorities established by Parliament, which is capable of providing redress for those with a grievance.

Journalistic standards, inherited originally from the press, have insisted on the primacy of accuracy in reporting what has happened. Yet there is nothing intrinsic in the process of broadcasting which ensures accuracy or fairness or impartiality. On the contrary, all over the world governments, military or police forces, political parties or extremists of a wide range, if they are in a position to obtain control of radio and television stations, often seek to do so for propagandist purposes. In Britain we are inclined to undervalue and take for granted what is familiar and so it is worth stating that truth in broadcasting is an ideal that can come near to realization. At the same time, experience elsewhere suggests that it can be eroded and undermined as easily, or perhaps more easily, than it can be directly challenged or overturned.

Constant vigilance is necessary to ensure that in news and current affairs programmes the overriding standard remains that of truth. Sectarian interests are strong, but they must be resisted. (Governments too are capable of exercising the most extreme pressures, sometimes claiming that the public good is at risk. There may be occasions when wider national interests should impose a limitation in news reporting, for example in the way terrorist incidents such as kidnapping are handled, but they are fortunately very rare and neither administrative convenience nor political advantage are sufficient justification for a departure from normal standards.) Whereas all this is easy to assert in general terms, and meets with little challenge, it is very much harder to carry out in practice.

V

Apart from news and current affairs there is the entirely separate issue of the advertising of consumer products and services on television and radio. Outside advertising circles this is an aspect of broadcasting policy that has received little comment in the years since the passing of the Television Act in 1954. Despite the dire predictions made by the opponents of commercial broadcasting at the time, advertising on television has shown itself to be unexceptionable in social terms, and highly effective as a way of communicating with a mass audience. The most telling vindication of the value that is placed upon television advertising is that one of the largest advertisers on television today is the Central Office of Information. The COI, a public agency financed wholly by public funds, acts on behalf of government departments in sponsoring a wide variety of campaigns ranging from energy saving to road safety; from recruitment for the Armed Forces to the prevention of accidents in the home. This has been the case for some years irrespective of whether the government has been Conservative or Labour controlled.

Because of its controversial origins Parliament insisted on safeguards being built in from the start. Not only was the amount and distribution of advertising limited, but the IBA, then known as the Independent Television Authority, had placed upon it a statutory duty to draw up a Code of Advertising Standards and Practice and to ensure that the code was complied with. This code had also to be reviewed from time to time, and the Act provides for the Authority to be advised in relation to advertising standards by a special statutory committee called the Advertising Advisory Committee. The membership of this body is drawn from organizations in the consumer, advertising and medical fields. When changes are made to the code, the Authority is required to have consultations with 'the Minister' (currently the Home Secretary). Such consultations normally take place at official level, and by means of the Whitehall network of interdepartmental communication the Authority can be made aware of the views of any government department which might have an interest in a proposed change in the code.

The Code of Advertising Standards and Practice has been greatly developed since the 1950s and now represents a comprehensive set of principles designed to exclude from the broadcast media any advertisement which is likely to be misleading, harmful or offensive. Some categories of advertising merit specially detailed rules. One such is financial advertising in which viewers may be invited to invest their savings, or to borrow money or obtain credit in various ways. Because viewers may be induced to commit themselves to financial risk or costly obligations a special appendix to the code details a number of safeguards, and moreover permits only a limited group of advertisers to use the broadcast media for this purpose.

Children, too, deserve protection from the more extreme selling techniques which an advertiser might be tempted to resort to in an endeavour to promote his wares via television. Popular though adult programmes are with children, often more so than programmes specifically produced for younger viewers, advertisements raise different issues and need to be judged in a different light. Essentially the commercials seen on television constitute an ingenious series of invitations extended to a vast audience of potential consumers to buy something. In receiving such invitations children face the screen without the benefit of maturity or judgement. The code seeks to take account of the fact that the ability of children to distinguish between fact and fantasy will vary according to their age and personality. With this in mind precautions are taken so as to ensure that no unreasonable expectation of performance of toys or games is stimulated by the excessive use of an imaginary background or by special effects. In studying proposed advertisements put forward by advertisers or their agencies the programme companies and the IBA are concerned to study carefully any material which is likely to lead children to copy dangerous behaviour or encourage bad manners. Certain forms of advertisement, for instance the permitted advertising of alcoholic drinks or tobacco products are kept away from programmes made specially for children, while advertising that may frighten or deal with subjects unsuitable for children is kept to later viewing hours.

Medical products can be advertised on television but their handling requires special care. Ever since 1954 the successive Television Acts have contained special provisions relating to 'the advertising of goods and services for medical or surgical purposes'. The British Medical Association and the Pharmaceutical Society of Great Britain are represented on the IBA's Advertising Advisory Committee, as is the Proprietary Association of Great Britain which represents the manufacturers of medicines sold over-the-counter. Under the IBA Act, any advertisement which makes claims about medicines – or about any matter affecting health or nutrition – needs to be the subject of advice from a member of the statutory Medical Advisory Panel. On this body serve a number of experienced consultants in general medicine and in dentistry. Since practical deeds count more than words, even when contained in Acts of Parliament, it is worth pointing out that restrictions include a ban on an appearance by doctors, or by actors impersonating doctors, in promoting proprietary medicines or any other medical products. Nor can outright cures be claimed, only relief. It is in questions concerning the rate and extent of relief that many of the most difficult questions of interpretation arise. No claim for tonic effects may be made, nor can there be any appeal to fear.

Over the years an elaborate system of control has been built up whereby scripts for some 7000 proposed new television advertisements are currently submitted to the ITV programme companies each year, mainly by advertising agencies, in advance of production. These are examined by a central secretariat established by the Independent Television Companies Association to check that they meet the standards laid down in the code. Copy clearance is handled collectively in order to avoid duplication and to achieve consistency over the entire network of fifteen companies.

This process of scrutiny, in which ITCA staff work closely with the Authority's Advertising Control Division, revolves around the questioning of words or phrases proposed to be used in an advertisement; the substantiation of claims, if necessary by reference to independent experts for verification; checking the validity of testimonials and the identity of persons to be introduced by name; and perhaps most important of all, a careful consideration of the total impression likely to be given by the finished advertisement, in vision as well as in sound, whatever the stated purport or words used in the advertising message. The emphasis on the total impression is crucial, for the likelihood of offence being caused in a commercial is greater than in a programme, while the justifications are much weaker.

Most broadcast advertisements aim, above all else, to sell a product or a service. They may entertain and inform as well, but these characteristics are incidental to the main purpose. Moreover they are very short in duration requiring a condensation of the information contained, while advertisements are normally repeated several times. Whereas the audience has a choice of alternative programmes on the three channels, the viewer who is watching the commercial channel will seldom make a conscious decision to view the advertisements. They are seen in natural breaks between or within the programmes, and it is by the programmes that they are supported. In this respect advertisements on television differ from advertisements in newspapers. It is, therefore, right that their content should be subject to separate and stricter standards as regards such matters as bad language, sexual innuendo, nudity or violence. The programme makers' justification in the case of full-length broadcast programmes, particularly in plays and drama series, namely that certain scenes are necessary to the dramatic narration of a story, is not available to the makers of commercials, and most of them are content that this should be so.

In day-to-day practice little argument turns on considerations of this sort, although agency producers like any other toilers in the vineyard are not averse to trying to push the boundaries out a bit. In so far as there is a regular battlefield, skirmishes are fought more on the matter of claims of superior performance by one product over another and their verification. Here the system is that claims involving scientific or technical matters must be referred to independent consultants so that they can advise on the substantiation offered by the advertiser. For example, the evidence in support of a claim that a particular detergent can wash whiter, or otherwise perform better than another brand, will be passed to an appropriately qualified independent expert who will assess the evidence. Similarly, a claim that a certain type of oil will give increased mileage and greater petrol economy will not be accepted without the report of an automotive engineer. As a result of this vetting process on average some 80 per cent of scripts submitted for television advertisements are found acceptable. The remaining 20 per cent are returned to the advertisers or their agencies for amendment. This statistic seems to indicate a system of control which is broadly effective in interpreting the requirements of the statute.

Inevitably moments of friction occasionally arise when an advertiser or his agency wishes to make a statement in the advertisement time he has booked which the programme company or the IBA does not think it would be appropriate to broadcast. However, the system provides for discussion between advertisers and their agencies and ITCA, so that views can be exchanged, sometimes across a table with expert consultants present on both sides. ITCA or IBA reservations are explained to the advertisers and usually differences are resolved without too much acrimony. Very occasionally there will be a row, but it is seldom that differences cannot be resolved at working level. It is unusual for a chief executive of a programme company to become involved in a dispute of this nature other than in the rarest instances. During eight years as a managing director I only recall half a dozen cases at most in which I was personally approached by an advertiser or agency about the content of an advertisement or a decision not to screen a particular commercial.

Overall there can be little doubt that the system which has been built up constitutes an extensive and flexible measure of consumer protection. Essentially voluntary in its operation, it is backed by the force of a statute, and is closely supervised by a public authority. As such it is preferable to the less sophisticated approach of an outright ban on what is described as misleading advertising. Something on these lines has been advocated from time to time by the Commission of the European Communities, as well as by certain national politicians. This blanket approach, although sounding fair enough, takes inadequate account of the difficulties of defining what is or is not to be regarded as misleading. As so often before in British constitutional development it is custom and practice, or case law, which makes a sounder guide and strikes a better balance between the freedoms of conflicting interests.

Despite any differences of opinion on the surface, deeper down it is generally accepted that the rules controlling advertising on Independent Television, and their interpretation, operate in the interests of the ITV programme companies and of the advertisers alike, as well as of the viewers. If the claims made in only a few commercials did not deserve to be believed, then doubt would be cast on the others. If the content of a commercial was crude and vulgar it would cause needless, and unjustifiable, offence. This would be bad for the advertiser, bad for the ITV company transmitting the advertisement, and bad for the public.

VI

Moving on from such practical matters as the drawing up and enforcing of a code on advertisements, we come to the even more treacherous ground of public taste. Good taste and decency are abstract concepts at best, and it would be unrealistic to expect them to be at the front of the programme maker's mind. Nevertheless the original Television Act placed upon the authority a duty, which remains to this day, to satisfy itself 'that nothing is included in the programmes which offends against good taste or decency, or is likely to encourage or incite to crime or to lead to disorder or to be offensive to public feeling'. This provision has been broadly interpreted and some programme makers have gone so far as to argue that the broadcaster has an obligation towards the writer or performer which is so strong that only in the rarest cases is intervention justified between the performer and his public. This rather simplistic, although often passionately advocated, approach overlooks the interplay between writer and producer, director and performers, and in fact many others directly involved in the production process, up to and including departmental heads, agreeing with each other or arguing with each other over how a story or a scene should be presented.

It is seldom possible to say what does or does not constitute an act of censorship. More often an intervention, whether on the part of the broadcasting authority or the programme management, and brought about as a result of unease or external representations, will favour one line against another, although each may have a considerable body of support in the production team. Circumstances will vary greatly from one incident to the next. But it sometimes seems to be the fact that a decision on content has been taken outside the production team that is resented more than the actual decision itself. Yet the justification for such intervention is clear. However highly the integrity of the individual producer or programme maker rates within the broadcasting organization, there will be occasions when it cannot be left entirely to his decision whether or not his own programme offends against an interpretation of good taste or decency or might be offensive to public feeling. To expect an impartial and dispassionate view from someone so closely and personally involved in a production would be unrealistic. Moreover it is on the broadcasting authorities that legal obligations have been placed in exchange for the right to broadcast and it is for these bodies, the BBC and IBA, in conjunction with the relevant programme managements, to see that they are carried out.

In a provocative lecture in 1979 Conor Cruise O'Brien pointed to a tendency he detected in liberal minds to identify freedom of broadcasting with freedom for individual broadcasters:

Such an identification would blur out of existence the distinction between a collective freedom defined by law, and a freedom taking the form of a licence to a limited number of individuals to use the limited number of channels available on the air-waves in whatever ways their individual judgements may dictate.

The concept of a limited number is of central importance here. It is because of a limited number of channels available that it has been accepted, in all democracies, I think, that fairness as regards broadcasting requires allocation, licensing, and specific regulation by law, and that the matter cannot be left entirely to private enterprise and the free play of the market (subject only to general laws applicable to all citizens) as is the case today with our free competitive press.

In the nature of broadcasting then, a limited number of people operating a limited number of channels enjoy direct access through image and through word to virtually the whole sentient population within their range. The general or partial establishment of new conventions, eroding public control over that access and conferring on the professionals who enjoy it a kind of arbitrary power, would thus be a social event of considerable magnitude and – on my argument – of sinister potent.[12]

In the world outside the broadcasting organizations standards of taste and public expression have undergone a vast change. Things are said and done by way of public performance that were unthinkable twenty, or even ten, years ago. The theatre, the cinema and the novel, each influenced more by the written word than by visual methods of presentation, have been in the forefront of the revolution in taste. Perhaps it is as well to reflect that the ability to withstand shock and to permit dissent from the established orthodoxies of the day historically has been the mark of confident and relatively prosperous societies. At the same time, the frankness – a less emotive word than permissiveness – of much contemporary theatre, cinema or literary writing is largely confined to selective audiences. These audiences select themselves partly by age, being mainly adult, and partly by the fact that payment is required as a condition of access by the public.

Two other factors distinguish these media, superficially comparable with television, from the broadcast media. The first is that the audiences reached by television are vastly greater in number and more widespread in nature. 98 per cent of all homes in Britain have a television set, which is switched on for between four and five hours on average every day. Not only do the audiences include old people and younger teenagers, but research studies indicate that these categories are amongst the heaviest users of television. Moreover, unlike any other media, television has an obligation, recognized by law in the case of ITV and by charter and long established convention in the case of the BBC, to serve a larger public interest. Thus it is clear that television has a responsibility in matters of taste which is different from that of any other medium.

How then does a man of conscience, making his legitimate career in television, recognize and evaluate public taste? It cannot be a formalized process. There are no concrete rules of guidance. Few executives, if any, sit down at their desk saying to themselves, 'Now let me think, what is the public concerned about today?' Letters from viewers and from special interest groups, representations from organized bodies, as well as newspaper and magazine writing about television programmes, add up to a powerful influence on the day-to-day decisions which are taken. No one should underestimate the effectiveness of a well-written letter addressed by a private viewer to the chief executive of a broadcasting organization about a programme which has attracted applause or criticism. In the case of the ITV Companies there are regular meetings between the companies and the Independent Broadcasting Authority at which general issues of public taste, often supported by research findings, can be considered at some length.

Significant though all these factors are, most important of all is the day-to-day dialogue that goes on between management and producers, producers and script editors, script editors and writers, writers and directors, directors and performers. This jumbled-up process, in which unconscious influences from the home environment and professional experience combine to shape the way an idea reaches the screen, is essential to any sort of creative organization. Every decision on what should appear in programmes, and the way in which controversial themes are handled, cannot be controlled on a day-to-day basis from above. The idea that any public authority or board of directors can declare there must be no falling off from standards, nor any reduction in programme quality, and expect results to flow from this dictum is unrealistic. No one ever set out to produce a bad programme. The whole skill is to establish and maintain an organization in which common standards are set and values accepted. That is where professionalism, in some ways so limited as an occupational philosophy, comes into its own.

VII

The most sombre question that cannot be avoided, and must be faced by programme makers as well as by the broadcasting authorities, is that of violence in television programmes. Stripped of all its qualifications the fundamental question comes down to this: 'Do scenes of violence on television contribute to violent behaviour, or attitudes which tolerate violence, on the part of individual viewers?' It is not a new subject for concern, having previously been asked of most other media, such as comics, films or radio, and no clear and unambiguous answer has yet emerged. Nevertheless, for the reasons cited earlier, television is characteristically different from each of these media.

A great deal of research has been done, much of it in response to the demands of public opinion, on the subject of violence. In America there was the Surgeon General's report on television violence in the USA, and the various reports and studies commissioned by the National Commission on the Causes and Prevention of Violence. This monumental enquiry, under the chairmanship of Dr Milton Eisenhower, was set up by President Johnson in 1968 following the assassinations of Dr Martin Luther King and Senator Robert Kennedy. In approaching this task the commission was directed to 'go as far as man's knowledge takes' it in searching for the causes of violence and the means of prevention. It did not spare itself in the thoroughness of its approach.

In Britain, too, there have been a number of studies, especially a notable series carried out under the aegis of the Centre for Mass Communication Research at Leicester University. The origins of the centre lay in a Committee on Television Research established by R. A. Butler as Home Secretary in 1963, and financed by the Independent Television Authority which made available a grant of £250,000 over a five-year period. The committee had as its purpose the initiation and co-ordination of research into television as a medium of communication and set out to study, in particular, the development of social attitudes and the moral concepts of young people under the impact of television. In 1969 the committee submitted a report to the Home Secretary summarizing the results of the research it had initiated and making recommendations for the future.[13]

The Leicester research studies concentrated on investigating the wider social implications of television rather than seeking to identify any direct causal relationship between the viewing of television and delinquent behaviour. But one feature stood out. This was the fallibility of the notion of the television audience as a sort of monolithic and cohesive entity responding to influences like some great jelly, swaying sometimes this way, sometimes that. On the contrary, the research findings underlined what common sense and personal observation already indicated, namely that the audience is composed of the sum of large numbers of people bound together only by the coincidence of watching the same programme at the same time. While there can be an element of shared experience, as for example when a political leader is speaking on a matter of current national importance, or when *Coronation Street* or *Crossroads* form part of day-to-day conversation with the neighbours, television viewing is essentially a private experience to which different individuals will react in different ways. This point was made succinctly in the summary of research results contained in *The Second Progress Report and Recommendations* of the Television Research Committee which stated: '. . . individuals brought to the viewing situation a range of differing interests, beliefs, concepts and levels of knowledge, and these acted as filters through which the programmes were viewed'.[14]

The work at Leicester continued after the Television Research Committee had been wound up, being succeeded by a Centre for Mass Communication Research at the University. Under the energetic direction of Professor James Halloran, the original secretary of the committee, this Centre has built up an international reputation. The BBC with its own audience research department has also carried out a substantial volume of social research, including a report on *Violence on Television*[15] in 1972. Other recent publications are *Television Violence and the Adolescent Boy*[16] by Dr W. A. Belson and *Sex, Violence and the Media*[17] by Professor H. J. Eysenck and D. K. B. Nias, both published in 1978. More generally Professor Halloran, in association with Mr P. Croll, was commissioned by the Annan Committee to describe research findings on broadcasting and his interesting paper, including a content analysis of violence in drama, news and current affairs programmes, was published as an appendix to the Annan report.[18]

If a researcher proficient and knowledgeable in this field were to be asked to summarize the overall conclusions of all this research, his answer would in all probability be evasive. He would point to controversy on technical and scientific grounds about the methodology and logic involved, and would explain that in any event not all of the findings are in agreement. He would say that in recent years there has been a move away from the search for evidence of direct effects on behaviour, although there was a mass of data to justify the assertion that television can be a significant socializing influence. While individual values and judgements may to some extent be influenced by the picture of the world acquired from viewing television, or indeed via any of the other mass media of communication, this process of socialization – or conditioning as some would have it – blends with the more immediate socializing factors of the family, the workplace and everyday life.

Violent action is undoubtedly a conspicuous feature of fictional television programmes, as it is in the cinema, while unhappily the real world outside only too often provides scenes of brutality and horror recorded in news programmes which surpass fiction. While it would be wrong, as well as shortsighted, to dismiss the possibility of any connection between exposure to portrayal of violence and subsequent violent acts, research so far has not uncovered proof of any direct causal connection. The most that can be said is that through a multiplicity of influences, social and personal, the mass media may in certain circumstances, with certain people, create the possibility of violent or delinquent behaviour which might not otherwise have existed.

Consequently research into the vexed subject of violence on television, important though it is as a contribution to knowledge, is unlikely to take the matter much further. Nor are the overwhelming majority of programme makers, whether working for the BBC or in ITV, generally either aware of or particularly interested in the conclusions of such research. What effects them, and what acts as the controlling mechanism in the studios where the programmes are made, is the extent to which violence is permitted on the screen and the justification for the inclusion of any scenes of violence. This brings us back to questions of editorial judgement, and here the editorial judgements of producers and programme managements are buttressed by guidelines. For some years ITV has had a set of codified guidelines, which are regularly reviewed, covering such matters as the context in which violence occurs in television programmes, whether factual or fictional; its intensity; its potential effect on children; and an outright ban on violence for its own sake. The ITV code is concise and is a key document for the understanding of the way in which this very difficult issue is handled in practice. It is reproduced in full in Appendix II. The BBC also has well-established guidelines in the form of advice to producers which has been supplemented and strengthened as a result of the report of a committee on this subject chaired by Monica Sims in 1978. Both sets of guidelines were published jointly by the BBC and the IBA in February 1980.[19]

The portrayal of violence on the screen is a problem which is a constant worry for many broadcasters, controllers and programme makers alike. In any discussion it is the man who says he has just given an instruction to tone down the violence in an action series who probably makes the most significant contribution. Conflict, the clash of purposes and personalities, sometimes is a major element in drama that will take the form of physical violence, that is conflict at the point when blows are exchanged or weapons used. Above all it is the context in which violent scenes occur that needs to be examined, for resort to violent actions, like other cliches, can become a habit without real justification. For the controller it is necessary to weigh the integrity of the writer and the artist with the effect on the audience. Even in dramatic works of high seriousness of purpose, at some point the scissors may need to come out.

No one will ever agree when such control on content should be applied, since individual judgements differ. Stormy scenes take place within the broadcasting organization, public accusations may be made, the press becomes involved and tempers rise. But in the end the programme management, however sympathetic and responsive towards creative considerations, which as I have already argued is of central importance, has to take the final decision. Sometimes in ITV a company management may be urged in a certain direction by the Independent Broadcasting Authority. But it is always best if responsibility is shouldered where it belongs, and for the company which commissioned a programme to see it through to its conclusion. Apart from periodic outbursts over the content of an individual programme it is in the exercise of quantitative control, the sheer number of programmes which are included in a schedule in which acts of violence occur, that a sense of social responsibility can best be shown by all those who have a say in the content of what is broadcast.

VIII

Nothing matters more to the programme maker than the atmosphere in which he works. Almost any creative endeavour, particularly when groups of people are involved in working together, will benefit from a positive and encouraging climate of opinion. Confidence is often a frail plant and it needs the right conditions to flourish. Relations between programme makers and programme managements have already been referred to and these can play a large part in determining the climatic conditions which favour the best creative work, especially the very rare masterwork which is seldom predicted in advance. Today, however, noticeable in the broadcasting environment is another element, elusive to pin down precisely, but evident nonetheless. There are unmistakable signs of an erosion of the spirit in the air; first showing itself in production and technical staffs, but beginning to spread to creative people.

That this should be so is hardly surprising since broadcasting, like newspapers, has not been able to escape the pervasiveness of the national mood which has come rolling in like fog enveloping so many aspects of contemporary life.

This mood changes and shifts, but its constant elements seem to be formed of a combination of deep-seated frustration and resentment, merging with a sense of lassitude and lack of purpose. Achievement drives are blunted and find difficulty in focusing on appropriate targets. In its most overt manifestations the mood can be highly demoralizing and damaging. It can and does play upon the outlook of individuals. It limits the boundless opportunities for the positive expression of individual character and personality. It has a significant bearing on relations between individuals and groups.

In the workplace, where so much satisfaction can be gained, there are heightened tensions between management and the unions, often channelled into obsessive, time-consuming and at times destructive conflict. In ITV the situation came to a head in a lengthy and bitter dispute over increased wages and productivity which took Independent Television off the air for ten weeks during the Summer and Autumn of 1979. The ending of a long period of pay restraint that had lasted throughout most of the seventies certainly contributed to this protracted clash. But was it the only cause? Earlier free collective bargaining had brought many benefits to the staffs of broadcasting organizations, not least in the matter of pay. In ITV these have now been consolidated at average rates of earnings which, even allowing for the inconvenient hours that some people work, are in most instances well in excess of the national average. Earnings compare favourably with most outside occupations, and have led to demands for comparable levels to be paid by the BBC which does not have the resources to do so without cutting back elsewhere.

The broadcasting industry is not alone in facing severe tests in daily relationships within the organization. For managements it is a test of will, sometimes of endurance. For employees and unions it is a test of reconciling aspirations which now far exceed conditions and security of employment with what is reasonable and equitable. There is nothing dramatic to be done to remedy this situation. It is a complex one, and many of the factors which have caused it are external to broadcasting. But for progress to be possible, and for the difficulties to be overcome, as they can be and as they must be, it is important to recognize its existence. To do otherwise would be to run the risk of following in the footsteps of a medieval prelate in charge of a crusade. When asked how his men should distinguish between the Christian and the infidel inhabitants of a town which they had just captured, he answered in words that have gone down in history. 'Kill them all,' he replied shortly, 'God will recognize his own.'

While television is a well-paid occupation, with good working conditions and the capacity for above average job satisfaction, it is also to a large extent a first generation industry. In the case of ITV many people are still employed who were there at the start, twenty-five years ago. The passage of time and the achievement of increased benefits have contributed to a lack of mobility. During the seventies the turnover of staff in Independent Television as a whole has averaged little more than 6 per cent annually.

Whereas stability can encourage the development and practice of technical skills in the production process, a more rapid turnround and freer entry is desirable for the creative people, particularly directors and producers who are responsible for the way in which ideas are presented on the screen.

In her book *Schools for Thought*,[20] Mary Warnock, herself a member of the IBA, identified the ingredients of the good life as virtue, work and imagination. These are the qualities needed today in television as much as they have ever been. One more could be added: determination or perseverance. Without it the fog will close in, reducing the priceless opportunities, exhausting the spirit, and so greatly restricting the potential for creative work which breaks new ground ever reaching the screen. Television will not be free if it is allowed to slide into a syndicalist phase, in which seemingly endless group conflicts, however legitimate in their motivation, blunt enterprise and drain away energy. Energy of the mind is as precious as physical energy resources. It is needed to fuel creativity, and it too can be threatened.

5

Radio finds a New Role

Radio is the oldest of the broadcast media, and the simplest. The ear is the main source of information and, as a carrier of the spoken word or music, sound radio is direct and uncomplicated. Technically the process of broadcasting from studios or outside locations for reception virtually anywhere within the range of the transmitter has become more efficient and less costly. In recent years a wider audience has become available through the rapid growth in the number of car radios (numbered in millions) and the development of cheap pocket transistors. The remarkable situation has now been reached whereby there are more radio sets in Britain than there are people. The quality of portability more than any other single factor has helped radio to survive as a mass medium in the face of competition from television. It has also had a marked impact on the nature of programming as listening to the radio has become more and more an accompaniment to some other activity.

The golden age of wireless, as Asa Briggs called it in his second volume of *The History of Broadcasting in the United Kingdom*,[1] was from the incorporation of the BBC in 1927 until the outbreak of war in 1939. The establishment of the conventions of non-intervention by government in the conduct of broadcasting during the twenties and thirties, and the leadership of Reith, have already been described in Chapter 2. The growth of broadcasting and its popularity stood out as a social landmark of the era:

On 1 January 1927 the BBC employed 773 people. There were then 2,179,259 wireless-licence holders. On 1 September 1939 the BBC employed nearly 5000 people and there were 9,082,666 wireless-licence holders. To put the matter simply, in 1927 the BBC was still a small organization, catering for a minority, if a large and growing minority, of the British public. In 1939 the BBC was a large organization, and it was catering for a majority of the British public.[2]

In music and drama the BBC made a noteworthy contribution to the cultural life of the country. While the theatre and concert hall remained secure as the principal platforms for the performing arts, broadcasting diffused the prevailing culture more widely than ever before. In doing so it helped to set standards, both influencing and responding to public taste. It also greatly widened the opportunities for employment of writers, actors and musicians. The BBC's attitude towards religion was uncompromising; it firmly regarded itself as having a duty in its religious programmes, as in its general approach to the audience, to uphold the established Christian orthodoxies of the day. When war came, it was the independence of the BBC, and the editorial integrity of those members of its staff who were responsible for the news, that dominated all else.

Although the powers of the Postmaster-General were transferred to the Ministry of Information immediately on the outbreak of war in 1939, and it was not long before a senior Foreign Office official was appointed to keep a close eye on the overseas broadcasts,[3] the BBC was never taken over completely by the government. There were understandings and assurances that the BBC would pursue national policies as part of a co-ordinated war effort, as well as maintaining a day-to-day relationship with the Ministry of Information. But from the first the BBC's broadcast output remained under its own control. It avoided becoming a controlled and selective instrument of government propaganda. Both in home broadcasting, where the BBC acted as a prime channel for communication between government and the people, and in broadcasting overseas, the BBC retained a sense of patriotic objectivity with truth as the guiding criterion. This was especially valuable in broadcasting to the occupied territories in Europe where the BBC built up a fine reputation. In some instances the memory of these achievements has endured ever since and is something which has served the BBC well.

So radio, which meant the BBC as the sole instrument of broadcasting, had a good war. The new medium had entered a new phase and met a new challenge. The national system of broadcasting had proved itself capable of adapting to a grave and extended national emergency in a level-headed and pragmatic way. Especially at a time when newsprint was scarce and newspapers were thin in consequence, radio had informed the public accurately and calmly of the progress of the war. In so doing it had rejected falsehood and avoided the temptations towards misrepresentations or slanting the news in an attempt to obtain what might be regarded as propagandist advantages. At the same time radio provided the channel for Churchill's inspiring war speeches. Winston Churchill made about forty broadcasts as Prime Minister between his first speech on taking office as Prime Minister in May 1940, 'Arm yourselves and Be Ye Men of Valour', and the end of the war in Europe five years later. They stand out as milestones in the history of the Second World War, marking a coming together of the British people as a nation, cementing and promoting the feeling of common purpose which was so crucial to the pursuit of ultimate victory.

II

In the immediate post-war era radio remained the vehicle for the expression of national values and aspirations, but with the removal of the external threat as a unifying factor society became more divided. It is interesting that Beveridge, who had given as much thought as anyone to the structure of post-war society, had so little to say in his report of the Broadcasting Committee which was set up in 1949 under his chairmanship about the influence of radio as a social factor.

After a brief, and now questionable, assertion that 'Socially, broadcasting is the most pervasive, and therefore one of the most powerful, means of affecting mens thoughts and actions',[4] the committee went on to address to itself a series of constitutional and organizational questions turning on the fundamental issues as to whether or not the monopoly of the BBC over all forms of broadcasting should be maintained. With one exception they answered in the affirmative, although Selwyn Lloyd's dissenting minority report, as described in Chapter 3, was subsequently to prove closer to the course of events.

At the time of the Beveridge review radio broadcasting in Britain, as conceived and operated by the BBC, was at its highwatermark. Apart from the overseas services the BBC provided three main services for its listeners at home. There was the Home Service, a middle-brow, middle of the road service, broadcast continuously from 6.0 a.m. until 11.0 p.m. daily. This was supplemented by the more popular Light Programme, mainly devoted to entertainment, and broadcast from 9.0 a.m. until midnight. Between them these two services were calculated to appeal to 99 per cent of the listening public, with 63 per cent attracted to the Light Programme and 36 per cent to the Home Service. The remaining 1 per cent of the average listening audience was tuned to the Third Programme, a service described by the BBC as 'designed in general for the serious listener. It aims to broadcast, without regard to length or difficulty, the masterpieces of music, art and letters which lend themselves to transmission in sound.'[5]

Although its audience was relatively small, and the hours of transmission much less than the two majority services (approximately six hours a day), the Third Programme soon built up an intensely loyal following as a later generation of BBC management was to find to its cost when attempting to reorganize the pattern of radio services in the 1970s.

Each of these three programmes was national in the sense that it was planned for, and largely received by a unified audience not differentiated by locality throughout the British Isles. There were some regional variations, but they did little to detract from the essentially national character of the BBC networks. The first television programmes were centrally planned and produced by the BBC on much the same assumptions. Even when ITV arrived on the scene in 1954 it brought with it a mandate from Parliament to function as a new national institution of broadcasting. This took the form of a regulated system of commercial television, financed by advertising, set up to compete with the existing national institution of broadcasting, the BBC, previously in sole possession of the field. This arriviste quality of ITV has always stung the BBC – sometimes causing it to cling somewhat temperamentally to the idea of the Corporation as the primary instrument of broadcasting in the UK in circumstances when the claim is hard to justify. It was only later, and then as a result of mainly organizational factors (i.e. those relating to the way the programmes were produced) rather than social factors (i.e. those relating to the way in which the programmes were received), which led to the regionalization of ITV which has had such a profound effect on its subsequent development.

As attention shifted away from radio towards television, network radio settled down in the shadow of the new giant. There were still many worthwhile and important programmes listened to with interest, even with affection, by audiences which at times could be counted in millions. But the challenge and excitement of working in a new and expanding medium attracted many of the best minds and keen creative spirits away from radio (and other pursuits) into television. In an astonishingly short period of time the internal revolution was completed and it was the television programme makers and the television technicians who had become the elite cadre within the BBC.

Of course there were still many skilled and experienced broadcasters and producers working in radio, while the central administrative and technical services such as engineering, finance and legal services were spread over the two functions. Nevertheless for at least a decade, from the mid-fifties to the mid-sixties, radio gave a clear impression of a medium in decline. The causes of the decline are evident enough, but in retrospect, it is harder to see why the BBC did not make an earlier, more imaginative and more determined effort to break out in a new direction.

III

Within the BBC the possibility of introducing a service of local broadcasting had been the subject of study and discussion since the early 1950s. Frank Gillard, a noted BBC war correspondent

Radio finds a New Role

and destined to be the first Managing Director of BBC Radio, was a particular enthusiast. He visited the USA in 1954 in order to investigate the operation of small and economical radio stations directing their output at specifically local audiences. These stations were highly commercial in their approach, and were regarded very much as part of the local business community. But they did give a uniformly high priority to collecting and disseminating information about the local community. Their mode of operation was immediate and casual, the flow of information being aimed directly at the lifestyle and interests of the individual listener. It was all a far cry from the aloof correctness of the BBC.

Deep down a distaste for this approach to broadcasting, encapsulated in the phrase 'giving the public what it wants', was probably one of the reasons why the BBC was so slow to move towards local radio. Another was the alleged shortage of radio frequencies. Long and involved technical arguments, often involving international negotiation and agreement on the allocation of wavelengths and frequency patterns, held up progress for some years. Then another question arose: if there was to be a service of local radio should it be broadcast on the new VHF (very high frequency) wavebands allocated to Britain by international agreement, or should it be confined to the more readily accessible medium wave channels? Technical opinion favoured VHF, but the potential audience, initially at least, would be considerably smaller. VHF had certainly been slow to catch on; although transmissions on VHF had been initiated by the BBC in 1955, ten years later less than one third of the radio audience was equipped with VHF receivers.

Eventually the BBC decided in favour of a system of local broadcasting on VHF. Eight stations in selected areas were approved by the Labour Government as a pilot scheme in 1967 and at first it was envisaged that these stations would be largely financed from local sources. Indeed the then Postmaster-General, Edward Short,[6] went as far as to tell the House of Commons that he had received 'a great many applications from cities throughout the country, in most cases agreeing to provide all the money necessary'.[7] This turned out to be wishful thinking, although at the time the reasoning sounded plausible enough. On behalf of the government, the Postmaster-General argued that since the essential purpose in launching an experiment in local radio was to give expression to local aspirations and interests, it seemed right that its income should derive from local sources. It would be unjust, he declared, to place the burden on listeners generally, for example in rural areas, for a new amenity that would not be generally available. If a community had a local radio station, then that community would have to pay for it in some way or other. The logic of this argument pointed towards local stations being financed by local advertising, but that was as far from the thoughts of the Labour Government as it was unacceptable to the BBC.

The optimistic belief that subventions from local public bodies would be adequate to finance a viable system of local radio was never well founded and it was not long before it collapsed in practice. Few in the BBC can have been as confident as the Postmaster-General, especially since the relationship between the broadcaster and his local paymasters could inhibit free reporting. And so it proved. In a revealing postscript to the history of this episode, the Managing Director of BBC Radio, Aubrey Singer, lifted a corner of the veil ten years later:

> The furthest (the BBC) were prepared to go towards some sort of local support was to accept grants from local councils. This worked until one local council objected to a bit of reporting to the extent that it threatened to withdraw its grant unless attitudes changed. The BBC immediately seeing the threat to editorial freedom withdrew from the council's embrace and henceforth all BBC Local Radio was to be funded out of licence fee except for certain 'one-off' capital subventions from local authorities.[8]

By the summer of 1969, with the first group of local radio stations launched, the government reluctantly accepted that if non-commercial local radio was to go forward the finance would have to come from the BBC's central funds, namely the licence fee. But a General Election was in the offing and consequently when the decision was announced that the BBC should go ahead with the establishment of up to forty local stations operating on VHF (the medium wave proposal to continue under discussion) it was made clear that this extension would have to be financed by the BBC from its existing resources until an increase in the licence fee which was to come into effect in April 1971. As Sir Charles Curran, director-general at the time, observed in his book, *A Seamless Robe*,[9] this was safely after the last possible date for the next General Election, which in the event came in June 1970.

Here then was one strand, chronologically the first, in the development of local radio: the BBC as a public corporation, still with a monopoly of radio broadcasting, seeking to extend its public service in a new direction. In the wings other forces, social and political, were gathering momentum. They were to influence profoundly the final outcome in the evolution of local radio in Britain.

IV

> So life was never better than
> In nineteen sixty-three
> (Though just too late for me) –
> Between the end of the *Chatterley* ban
> and the Beatles' first LP.[10]

Philip Larkin's *Annus Mirabilis* underlines one of the most remarkable cultural developments of the sixties in the shape of the demand, almost the craving, for pop music which manifested itself in a whole new generation of young people. Why this should have emerged in the way it did, at the time it did, is hard to say. It is likely to have derived, in part at any rate, from a weakening of restrictions within the family circle and the greater independence, including financial independence, of teenagers. The determination to do their own thing coincided with greater spending power. In turn this permitted increased mobility, allowing young people to get about more freely, to attend pop festivals and concerts in vast numbers and to establish contact at first hand with favourite performers and groups. Bernard Levin, in his portrait of the sixties, described it like this:

> The growth of pop music groups – many, no doubt, inspired by the gigantic commercial success of the Beatles

to believe that the lightning might strike them too, if they only formed fours and began to perform, but many, also, clearly in the business of self-expression – was the most extraordinary phenomenon in the world of entertainment of the whole decade; long before its end there were literally thousands of them, in Britain and America, and though many flourished only briefly, many displayed surprising endurance, and in any case there were always ten to take the place of one which fell.[11]

Advances in technology also played a part; the cost of long-play records came down; sales burgeoned and production of LP and EP records in the UK leapt from 26,926,000 in 1957 to 100,670,000 in 1964. Then there was the advent of the cheap battery-powered transistor radio, accompanying its owner everywhere he or she went. All these factors served to create a market. Radio, as the most pervasive and the cheapest means of disseminating music to a mass audience, was ideally placed to meet the demand. Yet with a few peripheral exceptions such as Radio Luxembourg, the American Forces Network and Radio Manx in the Isle of Man, it failed to do so. Despite some internal dissent by its bolder spirits, BBC Radio at the time was too set in its ways to react positively, and was insufficiently oriented towards responding to the needs of a mass public. Nor was the Labour Party, in government since 1964, prepared to contemplate the possibility of introducing commercial radio.

Into this vacuum, for the first time in British broadcasting history, entered a number of buccaneers, unlicenced entrepreneurs who set up a series of what came to be known aptly as pirate stations. These were transmitters located on ships, or other forms of off-shore floating platforms, or on abandoned forts in the Thames estuary. The best known stations included Radio Caroline, Britain Radio, Radio 390 and Radio London, but there were many others. The more successful of them quickly built up substantial audiences for continuous programmes of pop music introduced by disc jockeys who emerged as popular cult figures. These stations were certainly unauthorized in that they appropriated wavelengths allocated to other users by international agreement. They also caused interference with foreign stations and sometimes their transmissions spilled over into frequencies used by coastguards and shipping. But until the law was changed in 1967 it was not clear whether or not they were actually illegal since most of them operated from beyond territorial waters and consequently fell outside the jurisdiction of the British courts. The pirates also made extensive use of copyright material without making appropriate payments to copyright owners.

It was inevitable that the law should be changed, and in due course the loophole was effectively blocked by the Marine Broadcasting (Offences) Act which was passed by Parliament in the Summer of 1967. This statute made it an offence for any UK citizen to operate broadcasting apparatus on the high seas from any ship or floating structure, or to broadcast from an aircraft, regardless of the country of registration of the ship or aircraft. Equally important, it became an offence for any third party to collaborate with or support off-shore broadcasting by way of supplying fuel for generators, or other necessary goods, services or materials, including advertisements. This latter prohibition in particular caused the source of revenue to cease with the result that the pirates soon vanished from the scene.

Yet in their short and spectacular life the pirate broadcasters' output had proved immensely popular. The BBC now responded, if tardily, by finding the necessary wavelengths to launch a new national programme of pop music on 247 metres medium wave, initially called Radio 247, later rechristened Radio One. Even the name was derivative of the pirates and it was evident that for the BBC the whole unwelcome episode had acted as a lever, releasing the energies of some of the more enterprising of its staff who wished to break away from the stuffy image of sound broadcasting and make a determined attempt to staunch the flow of listeners away from the established services.

It was evident in the debates on the Marine Broadcasting Bill that there was a clear divide in the way the two main parties in Parliament accepted the need for orderly regulation, but while the Labour Government thought of the future in terms of an extension of the activities of the state broadcasting corporation, Conservatives were increasingly attracted by the possibility of finding a new way of fulfilling the popular demand which had been manifestly demonstrated by pirate radio. While no government could have permitted the pirates to continue to flourish, there was almost a kill-joy relish in the way in which the Postmaster-General introduced the measure terminating their existence: 'We in the House have a duty . . . to ensure that this unwarrantable nuisance which is being perpetrated in waters round our shores is removed as soon as possible.'[12]

True the BBC's new Radio 247 would take up some of the demand, and true also that the first faltering steps of experiment with local radio had finally been authorized. But local radio did not fit easily into the essentially centralized pattern of BBC broadcasting. Nor were any of the existing BBC services reduced, although the inadequacy of the licence revenue as a base for further expansion was already becoming evident.

These considerations led a body of opinion in the Conservative Party, including the then Opposition front-bench spokesman on broadcasting, Paul Bryan,[13] to think again about the possibilities of local commercial radio. Throughout the sixties there had been a steady lobby financed by radio manufacturers and other industrial interests, but the Conservative Parliamentary Party had not embraced it officially. Now, however, particularly since regulated commercial television had shown itself to be both responsible and popular, it seemed to point the way ahead. Significantly too a body of authoritative technical opinion was beginning to challenge the long-held assertion of BBC engineers that there were simply not the wavelengths available for any expansion of radio broadcasting. This radical view was supported by the findings of a survey carried out by management consultants, Urwick Orr, which had been commissioned by Paul Bryan and backed by some well-disposed businessmen.

Socialist distaste for commercialism and suspicion of the motives of those who spoke in favour of commercial radio persisted, although the public debate was nothing like as heated or acrimonious as that which preceded the introduction of commercial television in the fifties. And while the arguments for and against the BBC's monopoly and the widening of choice remained the same, the necessity to find a viable way of financing any extension of broadcasting loomed larger and larger as time passed. In the event, a pledge to introduce an alternative radio system financed by advertising was included in the manifesto on which the Conservative Party fought the General Election of 1970.

After the Conservatives had won the election Christopher Chataway, well known as a broadcaster, as well as a rising star in the Parliamentary party, was appointed as Minister of Posts and Telecommunications, the office of Postmaster-General having disappeared in a reorganization of the Post Office in 1969. As a first step he froze the BBC's plans for any further local radio development, and made clear that the new government would implement without delay its declared policy of introducing as many independent local radio stations as possible. For a time it looked as though the government might urge the BBC to withdraw from local radio altogether, concentrating its limited resources on network radio as well as its two television channels. But in the end, as Sir Charles Curran recorded:

> Mr Chataway decided that the 20 stations already opened by mid-1970, operating at that time on VHF, should be allowed to continue, and with a medium wave day-time supplement. For the BBC that represented a considerable political success in adverse circumstances, even though the twenty stations constituted only the half-way stage in the original full national plan.[14]

Meanwhile a plan for commercial local radio was taking shape. The architect of Independent Television, Sir Robert Fraser, recently retired as ITA director-general, was brought in to advise the Minister. Up to sixty local stations were envisaged, broadcasting on medium wave, to be financed by the sale of advertisements. The Sound Broadcasting Bill was vigorously debated in 1972, with some filibustering in committee where once again any extension of commercial broadcasting was opposed by the Labour Party. Most of the fire, however, had gone out of the issue and there was no repetition of the Parliamentary storms which had preceded the passing of the Television Act in 1954. That this was so was largely due to the fact that the evils of sponsorship on the American pattern, which had been so widely forecast, had been avoided in Independent Television as a result of adopting the system of a limited number of spot advertisements contained in breaks between and sometimes within the programmes. Both the amount and the content of advertising were subject to the controls exercised by the Independent Television Authority which were described in Chapter 4. Also all the indications were that controlled advertising of this sort was acceptable to the British public, and consequently a similar system was planned for independent local radio.

It was to the existing regulatory body, the ITA, renamed the Independent Broadcasting Authority, that the Conservative Government (although not without some hesitation) decided to entrust the new service of commercial radio. The question of a national channel financed by advertising in addition to the local stations was not ruled out, and in the early stages serious consideration was given to this possibility. In the event, according to Christopher Chataway, the main reason for dropping the scheme was that: '. . . It could have unacceptable implications for the national Press. It is for that reason that I came forward with a proposal for local stations only . . .'[15]

Press lobbying had not been confined to the national newspapers. The provincial press, fearing that local radio would hit its advertising revenues even to the extent of jeopardizing the survival of some regional and local newspapers, also had political clout at Westminster. Influential newspapermen such as Sir John Burgess, chairman of Cumbrian Newspapers and chairman of Reuters between 1959–68, expressed their fears to influential Parliamentarians, such as Borders MP William Whitelaw. As a consequence, the legislation, when it came, gave a privileged position to local newspapers in relation to local radio. If a newspaper had a circulation which, in the opinion of the IBA, represented a substantial proportion of the population of a locality in which the Authority proposed to establish a radio station, and the IBA was satisfied that the radio station would hit that newspaper's finances, then the Authority had an obligation to ensure that the proprietor of the newspaper was offered a shareholding in the station. Many newspaper groups were to take advantage of this prescriptive right to subscribe to the share capital when it came to the establishment of independent local radio stations. Almost a decade later, when both local newspapers and ILR stations were prospering, there was a certain irony in the fact that it was the same William Whitelaw, now Home Secretary, who told the House of Commons in December 1979 that the privileged position of newspaper groups would be discontinued in the application for future radio franchises.[16]

V

Once independent local radio was authorized it got off the ground without delay. An experienced former journalist and broadcaster, John Thompson,[17] had been seconded to the Ministry of Posts and Telecommunications for nine months while the Bill was still going through Parliament. He drew up a blueprint which, as soon as Parliamentary approval had been obtained, he was able to implement as the IBA's first Director of Radio. Contracts were advertised and a series of public meetings held as an opportunity for the expression of local opinion. At first there were doubters to be found even in the upper echelons of the IBA itself. Baroness Sharp, an eminent retired Permanent Secretary and a member of the Authority, admitted:

> I was one of the members of the Authority who . . . went round trying to choose some of the first companies. I then had no real confidence in Local Radio, and was not a great listener to radio anyway; but Mr Thompson fortunately had confidence enough for six and in due course he inspired me and indeed all the Members of the Authority to believe that there really was something here.[18]

The criteria adopted by the IBA in appointing companies as ILR contractors were first that they should so far as possible be locally owned and locally controlled; and second that their output should be both entertaining and useful. The word useful was deliberate. It implied an emphasis on radio as a utility as well as a source of leisure entertainment. If much of the programming was to be pop music, as it needed to be considering its antecedents, independent local radio aimed to become an integral part of the life of the community in which it was located. It was not content merely to coast alongside pumping out a routine of pop music, popular though that might be with many of its listeners. Thompson's plans, endorsed by the Authority with varying degrees of enthusiasm, were more ambitious. The local radio station, he believed, could and should be expected to establish itself as a principal source of information on matters relating to daily life. Traffic in towns, road works, the weather, job opportunities, news about forthcoming local events, market and shop prices, which chemists were open late at night, evening classes and Womens Institutes, what was going on in the local authority: it must have all seemed rather commonplace and mundane to broadcasters accustomed to more high-flown aspirations in the exercise of their mission to inform. Yet it was this emphasis that was to provide a new role for radio, an unexpected renaissance for the oldest of the broadcast media.

The first of the ILR stations, in London, Manchester, Birmingham and Glasgow, came on the air in 1973–4. Within three years nineteen were in operation, the maximum number permitted by government policy since the Labour Government on its return to office in 1974 had halted the development of local broadcasting while the Annan review was under way. From the start the stations adopted a style of cheerful, open informality. This breeziness became almost a trademark and it was one which reflected the vitality of the broadcasters. It arose partly from the challenge and sense of excitement associated with being in at the start of a new enterprise, and partly no doubt because several of the disc jockeys and some of the managers had learned their trade with the pirates.

As a by-product, local radio provided an outlet not just for the zest of those working in it, but also for their idealism. ILR made a particularly close contact with certain groups within its audience, including the elderly, the less articulate and the less privileged. Since it is exactly these groups in any community who often need help, but who are reluctant to get in touch with statutory or voluntary services, radio soon became established as a new and significant channel for social communication at local level. Moreover, an overwhelming majority in the audience were listening alone and were lonely. For elderly people and housewives spending much of their time at home, local radio came to represent a source of companionship: friendly, familiar and above all involved. For others the phone-in became a symbol of accessibility; proof that the local station was there to reflect the views and opinions of those who listened to its programmes, rather than leaving them to be talked at as was still customary on the more traditional radio services.

The social value of local radio's utilitarian role was dramatically illustrated during the exceptionally cold Winter of 1978–9. With severe weather conditions, including massive snowfalls, causing widespread and enduring disruption throughout many parts of the country, local radio stations were able to act as a primary channel for communicating advice and information to those in need. In 1979 the IBA published a report recording how:

> ILR stations around the country abandoned their normal programming and threw open the airwaves for emergency 'Snow Lines'. Some of the smaller ILR stations, serving predominantly rural areas, responded particularly well to the challenge, despite their relatively limited resources.
>
> Staff kept these stations broadcasting all through the night, often relying upon great personal effort (one presenter with Radio Forth, in Edinburgh, remained on continuous duty for 16 hours). Messages from stranded motorists were taken and relayed to worried relatives; there was constant liaison with the police and other emergency services to inform listeners about conditions; the organisers of events and activities cancelled because of the weather were able to pass messages to those planning to attend; elderly and handicapped people cut off in their homes were able to alert neighbours to their plight through contacting the radio station . . .
>
> Local newspapers were sometimes generous in their praise of ILR's role in mobilising the community, coordinating efforts to help those worst affected by the snow chaos. As the editorial of *The Scotsman* (4 January 1979) recorded: 'Radio Forth's "Snowline" programme, about which there has been a great deal of comment, was much more than an enterprising response to a particular local crisis or a useful service of news and information. It was also an echoing and spontaneous evocation of a society

still capable of mutual concern and compassion, and hungry for some focus for its practical expression.'[19]

Human nature too can rival the elements as a source of sudden disruption to normal living. Action taken in furtherance of industrial disputes by groups such as petrol tanker drivers, refuse collectors, hospital workers and ambulancemen, transport workers and employees of the electricity and water supply industries, have all caused dislocation and inconvenience to the public which depends on these services. Local radio, by broadcasting information about alternative arrangements and advice to those with problems, which are sometimes acute, can ameliorate their impact to some extent.

Apart from emergencies, whether natural or man-made, there is a continuing role for local radio to act as a focus for the practical expression of the concern and compassion which is latent in each local community. Stations have established close links with local statutory and voluntary agencies covering a wide range of social and medical care. The recruitment of volunteers has been a particularly fruitful area. Thus a severe shortage of blood-donors on Merseyside, for example, was alleviated by a campaign run by Radio City. This brought in over 2000 new donors living in and around Liverpool, while a half-hour outside broadcast by Pennine Radio in Bradford succeeded in finding over 100 new blood-donors for the Yorkshire Regional Health Authority. The same station was also responsible for recruiting 600 potential kidney-donors for the dialysis unit of a Leeds Hospital. Road safety, safety in the home, information on the prevention and treatment of hypothermia, adult literacy, health care, childbirth and child care are examples of public service campaigns which have been featured on ILR, with specialist advisers available to help over individual problems and queries. Exhibitions, conferences and printed material have served to back up the broadcast communication.

VI

Although the examples referred to above are taken from independent local radio there is no monopoly in virtue. The BBC's

twenty local radio stations aim to serve their communities in
very much the same way; indeed, being earlier on the scene,
they are entitled to much of the credit for pioneering a new
social, informative and community role for radio. Where there
is competition, particularly in the large cities, BBC audiences
are smaller, but there is no reason to think that the desire to be
of service is any less. Apart from the social motivation, however,
the BBC has two further reasons, more political in nature, to
stay in local radio. The first is the need to maintain a network
of local news-gathering points to underpin a genuinely comprehensive national news service. Although there is some force in
this argument, not too much should be made of it, particularly
since the BBC also has a series of regional newsrooms which are
used to cover some, but by no means all, out-of-London stories.
If local news-gathering points were to disappear, the regional
newsrooms might need to be strengthened to sustain a comprehensive national news service.

The second reason is less obvious but, in the curious way in
which public policies relating to broadcasting evolve, maybe
more important. This has to do with contact with leading
politicians. If a local ILR station is offering to MPs who are
also Ministers or front-bench spokesmen for their parties
regular opportunities to communicate with their constituents,
it is likely they will regard this as politically useful and accept
invitations as often as possible. If, having completed their
broadcast, they then meet the chief executive or programme
controller of the ILR station and some of the editorial staff, it
is likely that current issues of broadcasting policy will be discussed. Politicians are often more susceptible to atmosphere
than it might appear, and in this sort of relaxed setting many of
the preconceptions which later may have a bearing on policies
are formed. The BBC has always been sensitive to political
influences of this kind, and believes it cannot afford to sacrifice
such valuable contacts to its competitors.

Like many other British institutions in the public sector, the
BBC now faces an unavoidable dilemma in determining its
future policy towards the full range of its output in television
and radio. In an expanding and prosperous economy the ideal
course of action would be to encourage and support the new
while maintaining the old for so long as there is a demand for it.

But that happy state of affairs, so fundamental to corporate confidence and initiative, manifestly does not exist, nor is it yet in prospect. Consequently priorities have to be established and painful decisions taken.

The tides of growth and decline have effected radio profoundly over the last quarter century, in contrast with television which has experienced a relatively consistent pattern of growth. Soon the BBC will have to decide what to do about radio in the eighties. There is little chance of being able to carry on both with the old and the new. A choice will have to be made to concentrate resources on certain objectives. Either the existing national networks will have to be reduced in scope, or the growth of BBC local radio will be restricted. In practice it will probably be a mixture of the two, with little sign that advertising will be considered as an alternative source of revenue to the licence fee.

The present BBC output in sound broadcasting is substantial and varied. Apart from the overseas services (which are separately funded) and twenty local radio stations in England, the BBC operates four national radio networks as well as regional broadcasting in Scotland, Wales and Northern Ireland. Radios 1 and 2 constitute a service of popular music, although each is intended to have a distinct style and appeal. Radio 1, the original legatee of the audience inherited from the pirates in the sixties, is an overtly pop channel, while Radio 2 caters for all aspects of middle-of-the-road music. At various periods and at various times the two networks join together; and Radio 2 runs throughout the night. It is estimated by the BBC that between seven and nine million people listen, at some point during the day, to each service. Then there is Radio 3, broadcasting mostly classical music during the day supplemented by speech and some drama in the evening. Its daily audience is calculated at around 600,000.

Radio 4 is regarded by the BBC as a flagship, symbolizing its authority and tradition as a public service broadcaster. It is the principal channel for national and international news, as well as carrying extensive comment, interpretation and analysis of public issues. In addition Radio 4 broadcasts music, talks, programmes for women and young children, and specialist programmes for groups such as farmers and gardeners. There are also quizzes, comedy shows and other forms of entertainment programmes. It is the most expensive network to run and its audience, with some 4.8 million listeners tuning in each day, has melted away more rapidly than those of the other networks.

With the exception of Radio 3, which has been constant, listening figures for all of the BBC national radio networks have declined over the last decade. The causes are self-evident: the continuing pressure of television, particularly strong in the evenings; some diminution of interest in pop music by young people (allied to the growth of cassette recorders and players); and, probably most significant of all, the rise of local radio.

A wider view of the future, which will be greatly influenced by direct broadcast satellites and other technological innovations, is expressed in the next chapter. But for radio: simple, portable, and cheap as a means of communication, the trend can only be away from programmes aimed at national audiences in favour of a more selective approach towards particular interest groups in particular localities. The concept of regional radio, in England at least, seems already dead. Although a genuine attempt at devolution away from London, it satisfied neither local aspirations (the four BBC English regions each covered about a quarter of England) nor national needs. Television, being so much more expensive, depends on relatively large regions to generate the resources necessary for the full range of programme production. Radio does not, although much of the BBC's support for orchestral music has traditionally rested on a regional base.

Some reshaping in the pattern of radio broadcasting is probably inevitable. The BBC in Wales, for example, has enterprisingly gone one stage beyond local radio with an experiment at neighbourhood level.[20] This involved taking a mobile studio and transmitter to different towns for a period of four days each. During this time BBC staff encouraged maximum local participation in a broadcasting service devised by the producer on the spot to suit the individual community. This sort of travelling library approach, which has been successfully used in the Republic of Ireland, was well received and offers interesting possibilities for the future, especially in rural areas.

VII

The question that arises is whether all broadcasting, including small-scale ventures at local and community level, should continue to be planned and regulated by the two existing broadcasting authorities, or whether there is an opportunity for less regulation. For the BBC any expansion raises problems of finance: there simply is not any headroom left under the licence fee system. Moreover the BBC like the IBA is a national institution, concerned with national standards and responding to pressures applied at national level. It was for reasons of this sort that Annan, after roundly declaring that the organization of local radio was in a mess,[21] went on to propose the establishment of a new authority for local radio:

> We do so in the belief that local radio needs its own separate Authority, because local broadcasting is a different animal from network broadcasting and needs a different sort of keeper. Local radio has a quite different kind of relationship with its community, and the community has, and should have, an almost proprietary feeling about its local station that it cannot have about a national network. Networks are rightly looking for the common ground where people from all over the country can meet; local stations are looking for the village green where people from a single locality can be themselves and assert their separate identity. Networks do their job better as they broaden their coverage till they include the entire nation; local stations do their job better as they focus more and more sharply on a single individual neighbourhood.[22]

Although this analysis was generally accepted, and the ringing language applauded, the prescription was not. Its rejection resulted partly from audience loyalties expressed towards the existing stations, but more significantly from a feeling, evident even under the Labour Government, that there were quite enough controlling and regulatory bodies already and that the case was not made out for adding one more. The argument was thus about regulation rather than about the distinctiveness of local radio. Moreover, as the 1978 White Paper on Broadcasting had pointed out, local radio under the aegis of the BBC and IBA had been a considerable success. Consequently:

> . . . there must be a presumption against creating a new organization, with additional expense and bureaucracy, unless it can be clearly demonstrated that existing organizations are unsuitable for the purpose.[23]

If only those words were found more often in State papers, and the sentiment acted upon, how much healthier and more vigorous contemporary society would be. In the outcome local radio, its development frozen during the Annan enquiry, was confirmed as a permanent feature of the broadcasting scene and both BBC and IBA were given the green light to expand their respective services.

The next stage in the development of radio may be to work towards the introduction of a third tier below the existing national and local services. While it is difficult to draw a line between local and neighbourhood radio in terms of the type of service provided, there are substantial differences in scale. If the necessary money can be found from its licence revenue BBC executives have speculated on the possibility of up to forty-five or so local stations in England (including the existing twenty), each serving an area containing between 500,000–1 million people. These would probably need to supplement their local content by recourse to a sustaining service drawn from a reduced volume of network broadcasting. There might be a further twenty-five to thirty BBC stations of roughly similar size in Scotland, Wales and Northern Ireland.[24] Independent local radio can be expected to expand faster. It has the resources and the audiences to make possible the coverage of virtually the whole of the United Kingdom. Already forty-three stations are planned and there will be more in the future. Advertising has shown itself to be a secure financial base and it is likely that areas containing populations of approximately 100,000 should be able to support an ILR station with a reasonably wide range of programming. Stations of this size should have the capacity to broadcast up to 24 hours a day and have access to a certain amount of shared material, particularly in the field of national and international news on the pattern of the service already supplied by Independent Radio News. The possibility might be explored of subscribing to the same network services as the BBC in return for the payment of a fee which would help to finance network radio and enable it to act, in part at any rate, as a backbone service for local radio.

Below this level of local broadcasting, basically an extension of the present system, the opportunity exists for the introduction of small-scale radio. Estimates differ, but if the capital costs of setting up a station were kept to the minimum, and the hours of broadcasting limited to three or four a day, it should prove economic and practical in terms of wavelengths to operate radio stations in communities with populations of between 10,000–100,000 people. Such stations would almost certainly have to look to advertising as their main source of revenue, but if local newspapers, which are more costly to produce, can survive with circulations in this range, as they do, the indications are that radio could do the same.

The framework of regulation should be minimal. Some form of licensing, probably by the Home Office which already has both a Broadcasting Department and a Radio Regulatory Department, would be necessary, if only to prevent duplication and overlap with other authorized users of radio frequencies such as the police, radio cabs, air traffic, coastguards and the Armed Forces. But the tight control of ILR and BBC local radio stations by their parent authorities need not automatically be applied to neighbourhood radio. Even if it were thought desirable to extend the present system of controls, the reality is that no national body could be expected to have the sort of knowledge necessary to regulate such a diverse and plural form of local activity.

The case is overwhelming for permitting, indeed for encouraging, new local initiatives in sound broadcasting. They should be kept as free as possible from central controls. A plan on these lines would build on the success of local radio, allowing still readier access for those with something to say. It would also afford individuals and groups with a further channel for communicating with each other in a direct and personal way. At a time when so many forces in society work in favour of the mass rather than the individual, this is a valuable end in itself. As a utility, radio can be used to supply a flow of detailed information

.

about the daily life of the community, and to set it in its relationship to the surrounding area. In so doing it can help to strengthen the all-important sense of neighbourhood – the human desire to belong, not just to a place, but to the people who live and work there. In this respect radio has a social role different from television. It is one that should be built on in the future.

6

Institutional Broadcasting:
The Final Chapter?

I

When social changes coincide with fundamental advances in technology, political institutions are always likely to be threatened. All institutions have their foundations rooted in certain commonly held assumptions. If these cease to be commonly held, then the foundations will no longer be secure. One of the central assumptions in public policy towards broadcasting from the twenties onwards has been that radio frequencies, which are also used to carry television broadcasts, are in short supply and represent a scarce national resource to be husbanded and employed only for such purposes as the State decides. Some frequencies are allocated for broadcasting, while others are retained for a multiplicity of communication purposes between particular users such as defence systems, air traffic control, coastguards, the police and other land mobile users including ambulances, radio cabs and the fire brigade. In this country and elsewhere responsibility for broadcast programmes has traditionally been linked with responsibility for broadcast transmissions. In effect this is the basis upon which national control, which ultimately means political control, depends.

Since radio frequencies do not respect national frontiers an international authority known as the International Telecommunications Union (ITU) was set up as long ago as 1865. It now functions as a specialized agency of the United Nations and under its auspices lengthy inter-governmental World Administrative

Radio Conferences (WARC) are held in order to decide upon the allocation of frequencies to services such as radio broadcasting, marine navigation and links to satellites. One of the main purposes of these conferences is to minimize the adverse consequences of overlap and interference between applications in one country and another. Chaos in the radio spectrum has only been avoided by a pooling of sovereignty between member nations. This task is becoming increasingly difficult since 80 per cent of the world's telecommunications media is owned by only ten nations, with the whole of the Third World of developing countries controlling no more than 8 per cent. Thus the tensions and conflict which mark the international politics of economic development are already becoming evident in the allocation of radio frequencies.

The 1977 Satellite Broadcasting Conference in Geneva broke new ground and decided upon national allocations in the super high frequency bands (SHF) of the radio spectrum. These lie in the gigahertz range of thousands of millions of cycles per second, being the number of wavecrests which pass a fixed point, such as an aerial, every second. Their potential application is revolutionary, for they herald the era of broadcasting from satellites. Space satellites are already in use as a worldwide system of telecommunications links between ground stations at fixed points. These enable the transmission of a signal from one part of the world, or from space, for re-broadcasting by conventional terrestrial systems in any other part of the world where the signal is picked up by specially constructed ground stations. These telecommunications satellites are capable of being used to carry telephone and telegraph services as well as broadcast information. Satellites have a further dimension and it is one of great significance for the future. Not only are they capable of relaying pictures and sound over vast distances across continents, but communications satellites can also be utilized for direct broadcasting to the individual home. This facility will bring with it not just the prospect of a considerable increase in channels but, like the pirates in radio before, an entirely new set of issues relating to jurisdiction and control.

Direct broadcasting satellites, although confined to frequencies allocated to national users, will have an extensive coverage. The broadcast signal originates on earth from whence it is transmitted upwards to a platform suspended in geo-stationary orbit some 22,300 miles in space. From there it is bounced back again to earth via a transponder, radiating the returned signal like the beam of a torch illuminating the land surface which lies below. Thus a satellite intended to cover all of France, and to improve TV reception in the zones of shadow left by the existing French network of terrestrial transmitters, would also cover most of the South of England and part of the Midlands and East Anglia, at least for those enthusiasts who install the right sort of receiving equipment. Not all homes in the reception area would be able to receive the signal as they must lie more or less in direct line of sight to the satellite with no high ground or other obstacles, such as the house next door, intervening.

Homes would need to be equipped with a directional receiv-ing dish, probably of about three quarters of a metre in diameter, and to have an adapter fitted to the TV set. The receiving dish might be fastened either to the roof or an outside wall of a building, but provided it is unobstructed there is no reason why it should not sit out on the lawn like an overgrown sun-dial. In the initial stages the necessary aerial systems and conversions could be costly, perhaps amounting to some £200 or more per home until economies of scale and manufacturing improvements began to bring down costs. An alternative, particularly in urban areas, with high buildings constituting obstacles to reception, would be for individual homes to be linked by a cable system. This would permit the distribution by wire or optical fibre of a signal broadcast from a satellite and picked up by a single community aerial located at some central point. Apart from certain technical advantages cable distribution, being so much less conspicuous, is likely to be less open to objection on environmental grounds.

Even in the present preliminary phase of development each broadcasting satellite could provide at least five national tele-vision channels, including back-up facilities in the event of failure. A UK satellite poised in geostationary orbit over the Equator,[1] within sight of the UK, would be capable of covering around 98 per cent of the United Kingdom by land mass and perhaps something of the order of 90 per cent in terms of homes.

At present there are no plans to launch such a satellite, since Britain has not been as forward-looking as some of our European neighbours in recognizing the remarkable possibilities that exist. The reasons for this lack of interest are worth exploring, since they contain moral lessons on the way in which major political decisions are taken, or deferred, about the application of new technology and the implication for Britain's standing abroad, in particular within the European Community.

II

The first use of satellite communications agreed by the Extraordinary Administrative Radio Conference in 1963, namely an international satellite service linking earth stations at specified fixed points, was readily accepted and supported by the British Post Office. Its use as a means of exchanging simultaneous information, especially in the fields of news and sport, from anywhere in the world was self-evident. The telecommunications application loomed larger than the use for broadcasting since the demand for international telephone and telegraphic circuits continued to rise steeply, with satellite systems offering valuable advantages in terms of greatly expanded capacity as well as better technical quality and fewer delays. In 1965 the first communications satellite, known as Early Bird or Intelsat I, provided a facility for 240 two-way voice channels or one TV channel. The most advanced of the current series, Intelsat V, has a capacity of some 12,000 simultaneous two-way telephone circuits as well as two TV channels. An immediate application therefore existed which raised no great problems for decision takers.

In the direct broadcasting field the picture was less clear. The former Chief Scientist of the Department of Trade and Industry (and subsequently of the Department of Industry), Sir Ieuan Maddock, when addressing an audience of television engineers and executives in another context, described frankly a charactertic approach to new technology which has become all too familiar in recent years:

'Well we've done alright in the past chaps, we've coped in the past, why do we panic?' I've heard these kind of phrases from some other industries – the textile industry, the machine tool industry, the motorcycle industry, the TV set industry, the British optics industry – you've now got the British printing industry, and the pharmaceutical industry and agricultural machinery – all queuing up – for God's sake don't follow that. It's not unique to us, incidentally, the Germans have lost their optical industry and the Swiss have suddenly woken up and found they've lost their clock industry.[2]

Maddock argued that for advances in technology to be exploited successfully two conditions are necessary. There must be a pull towards new standards and new inventiveness, in the shape of a demand expressed by governments and other commissioning bodies, public and private, which constitute the potential users and ultimate beneficiaries. This needs to be matched by a push consistently applied by the suppliers of technology: the inventors, the designers, the manufacturers and the salesmen:

> The thing that has put America where it is is not the technological push of the IBMs and the Boeings and North American companies, it's the pull – from defence, from NASA, from the Federal Aviation Agency, from the Federal Communications Agency etc. who demanded and demanded because they had people who understood what was technologically possible at any time and who knew where the frontier was.[3]

The level of investment and the availability of resources come into the equation and will of course greatly effect the calculation. What is possible in the United States, the richest and most prosperous economy the world has ever known, compared with Britain in an era of post-Imperial decline, is very different in scale. But behind the practical implications of resources lies the all-important question of attitude. The American space programme of the sixties, with the objective of putting a man on the moon, was more than a scientific project. It became a national aspiration, almost a latter-day crusade. The by-products for technology were colossal and some of the benefits are still coming through. The silicon chip and microprocessor for example were given tremendous stimulus by the space programme and its spin-offs. Is it possible to detect the same drive, the same energy and single-minded determination in the way the British have approached much smaller, more realizable steps forward in technology?

Throughout the seventies there was very little interest in Britain in the potential application of the rapidly advancing satellite technology for broadcasting purposes. There were a few visionaries and futurologists who spoke and wrote enthusiastically about the exciting possibilities that lay ahead, but such interest as existed was speculative and not translated into practical studies. The Annan Committee reflected the prevailing mood. Although specifically charged in its terms of reference 'to consider the implications for present or any recommended additional services of new techniques',[4] the committee seemed to find it difficult to summon up any enthusiasm in addressing itself to this part of its mandate. No research papers were commissioned, although several were on other subjects, and the report itself devoted no more than three paragraphs to satellite broadcasting. These pointed out that while the advantages for international telecommunications were clearcut, the broadcasting application was likely to be of more relevance to countries like Canada and India where the purpose was to provide the same service to places thousands of miles apart.[5] In Western Europe, where the distances were much less, and the existing investment in conventional means of broadcasting far greater, Annan concluded it was unlikely that broadcasting satellite services would have any high priority for some years to come. With this observation the committee left the subject for their successors to tackle, perhaps in another ten or fifteen years' time, but not before declaiming: 'We consider it essential that broadcasting satellite services should be licensed and regulated in the same way as the present broadcasting services.'[6]

That was all. A flat statement: not reasoned; not tested by argument, at any rate as far as could be deduced from the report; and in all probability not tenable. Let there be no doubt about it, this is going to be the central question which will face those responsible for broadcasting policy over the next two decades until the end of the century. That there are significant technological developments already on the scene is now self-evident. Events have pointed towards a demand by the public for at least three of them: satellites, cable, and videocasettes and other home entertainment systems. Together they will combine to undermine the old familiar assumptions.

Future committees set up to review the state of broadcasting are likely to reflect ruefully on a time when such confident declarations could be made, presumably in the belief that it would be possible for national governments, whether by convention or statute, to continue to assert their power of regulation in a markedly different situation. What we may well be facing, and what seemed to escape the finer perception of the Annan Committee, as well as other commentators on broadcasting policy, is that there is little chance that the institutional future will resemble the past. Human nature may not alter very much, if at all, but the way people work together is conditioned by the tools at their disposal and by what is expected of them by their publics. Complacency may be too strong a word in this rather limited context, nevertheless it is true that most of us are more comfortable if our thoughts and actions are confined by the parameters of institutions we have learned to know and live with. Thus familiarity tends to take on overtones of permanence and institutions build up an instinctive resistance to the changes that may be called for by the altered climate in which they operate.

In a far-sighted and powerful speech at the end of a convention held by the Royal Television Society in Cambridge in the Autumn of 1979 John Freeman, chairman of London Weekend Television, put it like this:

> Are we perhaps wrapped in an imaginary cocoon of permanence? The advancing tide of cable, satellite and videodisc and combinations of all three, will not of course kill off-air broadcasting, even though it will lead to a very rapid development of narrow-casting. It may well however change almost out of recognition the present institutional forms. I do not believe that this tide of change will be stemmed for long. In the longer run public opinion simply will not allow this, once the techniques are readily available,

and I doubt very much whether the tide will be contained within the existing institutions. How much that matters to the public interest, I am not sure, but it matters to us as institutional broadcasters. I would only say to those . . . who see the public interest in broadcasting best maintained by structured institutions, that we had better give a good deal more thought to what lies ahead, and to give it urgently if we expect to adapt our institutions and structures to tomorrow's world.[7]

III

Measured against this yardstick, what has been the British response to the opportunities offered by the broadcasting satellite? In May 1975 the European Space Agency (ESA) was established, inheriting some of the functions of the European Space Research Organization (ESRO). Its stated aim was to promote, for exclusively peaceful purposes, co-operation between European countries in space research and technology with a view to their use for scientific purposes and for operational applications. These applications included meteorology, maritime communication between ships at sea and shore stations, telecommunications and direct broadcasting.

Together with the other members of the European Communities (with the exception of Luxembourg) the United Kingdom is a member and is represented on the Council of the European Space Agency by a senior civil servant from the Department of Industry.[8] Spain, Sweden and Switzerland are also members, with Austria, Canada and Norway participating in certain programmes. In 1979 the annual budget of the Agency was running at the level of about 684 million in US dollars. France and West Germany contributed over half the budget between them; their respective contributions expressed in percentage terms of the general budget amounting to 33.4 per cent from West Germany and 26.8 per cent from France. The UK share in 1979 was 11.7 per cent.[9]

The principal heads of expenditure were the Ariane rocket launcher (28.6 per cent of the budget), designed primarily by the French in association with the ESA, in order to provide

Europe with its own satellite launching capacity; and the Spacelab (taking some 22 per cent of the budget). The latter project, a manned orbital laboratory, is being developed in Europe as a contribution to the American Space Shuttle programme. These two projects, taken together, accounted for almost half the total expenditure of the European Space Agency. In addition to their communications and scientific potential both had weighty implications in terms of industrial policy and employment in France and West Germany.

Some subcontract work in connection with the Ariane launcher is being carried out in Britain, while British Aerospace Dynamics Group was a prime contractor in the consortium that built the orbital test satellite for the European Space Agency in the mid-seventies.[10] This was a pre-operational communications satellite which was successfully launched in May 1978 following an earlier failure in 1977. It is currently being used to prove the design and systems engineering embodied in a new range of European Communications Satellites (ECS) that are now under construction. Initially there will be two of these ECS satellites, although five are envisaged over the next ten years. Their main purpose is to act as point-to-point telecommunications links rather than for direct broadcasting. Each can carry up to 20,000 telephone circuits or 12,000 telephone circuits plus four television channels. Already French television is being beamed to Tunisia via the orbital test satellite.

In 1977 the European Space Agency, in conjunction with the European Broadcasting Union, held a conference in Dublin on the potential use of satellites for broadcasting purposes. At this meeting a plan was put forward for a satellite described as H-Sat (for Heavy Satellite) which would be a large platform in space capable of carrying a variety of payloads to radiate television programmes for reception in individual homes on earth. The costs were considerable, the system not proven, and only the Scandinavians with special problems of covering mountainous terrain by terrestrial means saw any advantage in pressing forward as a matter of priority. In fact national broadcasting organizations gave nominal support to H-Sat, but in the absence of any real determination the project failed to make progress and eventually was subsumed in a later programme, known as L-Sat.

Meanwhile other pressures, political and industrial, were bearing down on the European Space Agency as interest began to mount in the possible use of satellites for broadcasting. The leaders were France and Germany, two of the principal paymasters of the ESA and countries with large stakes in the manufacturing processes for the Ariane rocket launcher as well as for many of the satellite components. Export markets were opening up elsewhere in the world; the German space industry for instance being particularly interested in China. Before long a Franco-German accord developed that unless some action in Europe was taken, and soon, the market would be left for the Americans.

What happened next was an instructive lesson in political/industrial decision-taking. The Space Agency proved itself too slow and cumbersome a vehicle for the realization of the ambitious French and German aims. International bodies usually move at the speed of the slowest member and the ESA was no exception. Moreover, there were political reasons why it might be to the advantage of France and West Germany to work together on a bilateral programme in an area of advanced technology which promised so much for the future while employing so many of their technicians in the present. Thus after the French President met the German Chancellor at a summit meeting on 2 October 1979, agreement in principle was announced that the two countries would co-operate in the development of direct broadcasting satellites. The proposed co-operation had three aspects; starting with a pre-operational phase in which two identical satellites would be constructed with a view to being launched by the European Ariane launcher. An industrial phase would follow, details of which have yet to be worked out. A third aspect relates to the use to which the satellites would be put. The programme envisaged the joint development and manufacture of five identical satellites in all. It is probable that the German main contractor will be Messer-schmitt-Bolkow-Blohm (MBB) with la Société Nationale Industrielle Aérospatiale (SNIAS) taking the lead on the French side.

This decision left the European Space Agency with a yawning gap in one of its larger programmes. Direct broadcasting, it is true, is only one of a wider range of satellite applications, but it is amongst the most conspicuous and is highly charged politically. Whether or not the Space Agency's L-Sat project can survive without the support of France and Germany remains to be seen. The United Kingdom is currently supporting the definition stage and has undertaken to bear about 35 per cent of the cost. The estimated cost of the whole programme will not be known until the end of 1980 and at that stage Britain will have to decide whether to continue with its participation in the L-Sat programme, or to change course and opt for a UK broadcasters' satellite in the mid-eighties. In any event, the dilatoriness of our national approach in the past will ensure that the background against which the policy decision is taken will be characteristically negative and defensive.

Not only will the French and German satellites be in operation well before any system in which Britain is likely to play a part, but the smallest of the European states, Luxembourg, may already be on the field and in the game. With a long history of commercial broadcasting, first in radio and then in television, Luxembourg is a member of the International Telecommunications Union (although outside the ESA) and as such applied for and was granted by the Satellite Broadcasting Conference frequencies suitable for satellite broadcasting. In the past Radio-Tele Luxembourg has thrived, despite its tiny national base. That this should be so has resulted mainly from chronic French ambivalence towards the question of broadcast advertising on the State-owned channels. Consequently Luxembourg, with powerful transmitters reaching far into France and Germany has prospered, largely financed by outside commercial interests, as well as by the French Government. Now Luxembourg has the potential, if it should decide to make use of it, to launch one or more satellites, broadcasting popular programmes, probably with feature films as the staple diet, in English as well as in French and German, over a vastly larger area. Such a facility could be commercially attractive to Radio-Tele Luxembourg's backers, since the reception area for the programmes would cover most of Europe's so-called 'Golden Triangle'. This would extend over almost 50 per cent of French territory, including the prime Paris area, while in Germany the satellite would penetrate deep into the great urban concentrations of population in the Ruhr. Part of the south of England might also be able to receive transmissions from a Luxembourg operated satellite.

What has been discussed so far refers only to the public sector, that is future developments in space communication financed or approved by the State which are likely to have an effect not just on their own citizens but on those in adjoining territories. In the United States of America there are in addition several essentially entrepreneurial private ventures already in operation. These are expanding fast, for what has happened is that the availability of satellites as a means of delivering pictures and sound over the entire North American continent has coincided with the growth of some 2000 separate cable systems. In return for a monthly payment these provide subscribers with a better picture, which is important in America where the quality of reception is generally far below that prevailing in the UK, as well as a wider choice of between twenty to sixty channels.

The great increase in the number of available channels has led to a demand for material of all sorts. Satellite services relayed to cable systems already include pay television programming and feature films supplied by off-shoots of large entertainment groups such as Warner Brothers and Time-Life, continuous live coverage from the House of Representatives, special programmes for children and for sports enthusiasts, classical and disco music, as well as religious, ethnic and foreign language programmes, for example the Spanish International Network. The output of certain independent television stations, known as super-stations, notably WTBS from Atlanta, WGN in Chicago, WOR in New York and KTVU in San Francisco, is also distributed by satellite. Other commercial applications can be found in the syndication of news and the provision of satellite business systems. These continuing services are backed up by a growing list of specific corporate communications purposes such as the introduction to retailers or sales forces of new models of automobiles, or the launch of other nationally branded products.

Whether such high risk, high cost commercial ventures would flourish in the colder economic climate of Western Europe is open to speculation, although the opportunity and the technology to exploit it already exist. Certain crucial differences, moreover, exist in the institutional framework. In the United States, for example, satellite distribution channels are available at commercially competitive rates, whereas in Europe the monopolistic posts and telecommunications administrations have kept charges at an artificially high level. Nevertheless, the market is there, and a pull towards satellite communication will inevitably make itself felt before long.

IV

What other technological developments are on the horizon, or closer, which have a good prospect of taking root in popular favour? Cable systems have already been mentioned and, while not a new idea, their utilization in Britain is likely to grow rather than to decline as a result of the inherent environmental advantages (cables buried in the ground are less objectionable to environmentalists than forests of aerials sprouting up into the sky), as well as from technical improvements. The most significant step forward in the technology of cable distribution lies in some striking advances in the field of fibre optics. Small diameter glass cables have been developed to carry light. This can be modulated in the same way as an electric current to transmit television signals from point to point. The cables containing concentrated beams of light have advantages in that they occupy very little space in the cable ducts as well as costing less than copper wire. Moreover, they have intrinsically superior technical qualities such as freedom from interference by neighbouring electrical cables. Linked to community aerials, cable systems in built-up areas become an economic and socially acceptable way of delivering to the individual home a wide choice of television programmes from satellites as well as other visual information.

In the home itself it is likely that there will be, as is already becoming apparent, an increasing range of home entertainment equipment. A look at any teenager's most prized possessions will confirm the trend that has emerged throughout the seventies. Portable radios and audio cassette player/recorders will be complemented by stereo music centres, video cassette player/recorders and by video discs and players. Each of these video systems has the great advantage of using the screen of a standard television receiver for display purposes, although sometimes as in the case of the teletext services, Oracle, Ceefax and Prestel, an addition is required. There is no reason why inexpensive remote control units enabling a viewer to switch from one programme to another, or from one service to another without getting out of his armchair, should not become universal; while the screen of the TV set can be expected to become both larger and thinner until it can be hung on the wall like a picture. Some manufacturers of electronic equipment have produced physical mock-ups of combined home entertainment furniture. Apart from being somewhat elephantine in appearance, articles of this sort, built around a large TV screen of up to 50″–60″ (about double the present 26″ screen in size), and flanked by some smaller subsidiary screens, are hardly likely to be mobile. Since, however, the audience in the home is generally mobile and does not wish to be anchored in the living room, it is probable that most of the electronic equipment will remain as portable as possible, rather than being concentrated in a single unit. Indeed there are some engineers, wise and worldly men, who have grown sceptical of the claims of the visionaries over the years and believe that variations in the purchasing patterns of the existing generation of equipment are likely to make as much or more of a social impact on the audience as all the wonders of the new technology.

Probably both will be proved right to some degree. It would certainly be unwise to overlook the rapid growth in the number of households with more than one television set. By 1976 American estimates showed that almost 50 per cent of all homes had more than one set, and that in some large urban areas the figure was over 60 per cent.[11] This trend had been evident for some time; in fact as early as 1965 the present author, acting as rapporteur for a seminar organized by Stanford University in California, wrote an article for *The Times* titled 'American TV Considers the Viewer with Several Sets'.[12] Would the same pattern reproduce itself here? After all television sets are expensive items and the difference in the standard of living might prove decisive.

The figures quoted below are taken from Independent Television sources, but BBC or manufacturers' statistics would show a similar trend. In the early seventies JICTAR surveys indicated that the percentage of households capable of receiving ITV which contained more than one television set remained fairly constant at around 3 per cent. This figure then began to climb reaching double figures in some parts of the country by 1976. Thereafter the growth accelerated sharply. By April 1979 estimates indicated that 16 per cent of all ITV households, totalling more than 3 million homes over the country as a whole, owned or rented more than one television set. There were considerable regional variations in the figures, percentages reaching as high as 19 per cent in Wales and the West of England and as low as 7 per cent in Northern Ireland. Taking into account that the percentages are not offset by the substantial number of one-person households where a second set would usually be superfluous, the figures show a remarkable surge in popular taste towards greater selectivity in choice of programmes and greater privacy in viewing them. Expressed in numerical terms the decade saw an estimated 445,000 households with more than one set in January 1970 grow to a total of 3,067,000 households in April 1979.[13]

The implications of this phenomenon, in the same way as the impact of the new technology, are likely to make themselves felt both on the suppliers of programmes and the institutional framework within which they are contained. The response of the programme maker can only be towards programmes aimed more and more at appealing to the tastes and interests of individual viewers, rather than searching for common factors and common interests with the widest possible appeal to the family group.

Consumer purchasing behaviour of the existing range of electronic equipment, together with the extent to which the original set is retained in the home when a new model is bought or rented, will combine with the potentialities of the new technology such as satellites and cable systems to provide a wider choice for the individual. Scarcity of channels in the past has coincided with a single TV set in the home. Now both fixed points in the relationship between the broadcasters and their audience – the way messages are sent and the way they are received – are undergoing a fundamental upheaval.

On the face of it these are developments to be welcomed. They bring with them the promise not only of a wider range of choice for the individual viewer, but also a closer cultural identity in terms of communication between the provider of information and the user: between the sender, the message and its receiver. Both of these consequences are equally desirable and represent an extension of freedom; a move away, however imperceptible at first, from a mass culture in favour of one oriented more towards the tastes and values of the individual citizen. There are, however, some more sombre considerations lying only just beyond the present horizon.

The narrowing down of the process of broadcasting to more sharply defined focal points will be reinforced by the most promising of all the innovations outside the field of broadcasting. In December 1978 the video long-player went on sale to the public for the first time in a test market in the United States. This device enables a video disc, in appearance not unlike an ordinary LP gramophone record, to be rotated at high speed by a player which reproduces a colour picture on the screen of a normal domestic TV set. The system is not yet standardized, although the research and development originally carried out by more than twenty-five separate organizations in different parts of the world has come down to two alternative methods of reproduction, optical and non-optical. The first, now being piloted in the United States by Philips/Magnavox, is based on projecting a concentrated beam of very bright light in the form of a laser onto the reflective surface of the disc. This system has the support of MCA, one of the market leaders in the American entertainment industry with a vast catalogue of film, music and television material, as well as of IBM. The main rival to the optical disc is SelectaVision, a system with a diamond stylus head in physical contact with the disc. This has been developed by the giant electronics group, the Radio Corporation of America (RCA). RCA has among its subsidiaries the National Broadcasting Company which provides one of the three national TV networks in the United States, and also has access to substantial programme resources. It is anticipated that SelectaVision will be launched nationally in the US in 1981 where it can be expected to have a major impact. Other manufacturers, notably JVC in Japan, have been developing alternative methods of non-optical reproduction, but a majority of them may decide to wait and see which system prevails before coming into the world markets on a large scale. In the meantime, there are problems of copyright and royalties that need to be resolved, while the techniques of programme production will call for some adaptation to meet the requirements of a new medium.

When it arrives in Britain, in the next year or so on the manufacturers current projections, the video long-player will probably retail at a price somewhere between the cost of a 26″ colour receiver and a video cassette recorder (approximately £380 and £600 respectively at 1979 prices). In the United States the Philips/Magnavox player was selling in 1979 at $775, with the discs costing $24.95 for a feature film with a playing time of two hours, down to discs containing entertainment shows, sport or educational material with a playing time of 70 minutes (35 minutes a side) retailing at $19.95 and $14.95. The RCA system should produce a player that is cheaper, and in each case pictures and sound can be received via the normal domestic colour television receiver.

Video discs and players will have a price advantage over the video cassette recorders and players which are already generally available. Moreover, the video cassettes themselves containing magnetic tape for home recording or pre-recorded material are more expensive than mass produced discs.[14] The characteristics of the two systems, however, are markedly different and there should be room for both to survive. Experience of the existing market suggests that video cassette recorders are primarily used to record broadcast material in the home, especially at times when the viewer is not available to watch the broadcast live. The video cassette recorder can thus act as a time-shift machine, enabling people to watch the programmes they want to see at times convenient to them, rather than at the times they are broadcast.

V

These non-broadcast devices will supplement developments already apparent in broadcasting, but their effect on public broadcasting will be limited. They are described here, together with satellites and cable systems, because it is vital to have some understanding of what is involved in any new technology, what can be done and at what cost, and what the alternatives are, before considering the implications in terms of public policy.

In his recent book, *Arguments for Socialism*, Tony Benn made this point strongly:

> New technology and the way it is handled has other important implications for democracy. One of the frightening things about high technology is that, because it requires a high degree of scientific education in those who work in it, a new priesthood develops. The scientific community is inclined to say 'Oh, you don't know anything about this. It's all very complicated. You've got to do it this way' . . . If we fail to insist on explanations and adopt centralised or technocratic solutions, we will come unstuck sooner or later.[15]

Greater availability of frequencies for broadcasting purposes, and an electronic technology that has passed from the stage of invention to that of application, are shaping a future of which the outlines are just beginning to emerge. The public sector may be overshadowed, partly as a consequence of the pressure to reduce public expenditure, and partly because private interests will be seeking to exploit the potentialities of the technology by identifying groups of people with particular needs or desires and then supplying these requirements through the market place. A wider communications environment can be expected to bring with it more diversity in the form of more specialized programme material appealing to individual viewers, although paradoxically satellites will deliver a much broader choice of programmes to far larger audiences, often extending over national frontiers.

What, then, will be the impact of all this on the broadcasting institutions of the eighties and beyond? No one can say with any certainty, but it is as well to think about the implications in good time and not to regard the present arrangements as immutable once the assumptions upon which they rest are eroded. To restate the proposition advanced at the start of this chapter: the fundamental assumption upon which policies towards broadcasting has depended in Britain for the last half-century or more is that frequencies in the radio spectrum are scarce national resources. As such their use, whether for broadcasting or other purposes, should be regulated by the State. Control of the means of transmission has led to control of the programme making process, and of the way in which the programmes are presented to the public. It is this equation, lying at the heart of the finely tuned system by which broadcasting is controlled, that is likely to be undermined by a combination of technological and social factors.

The way policies towards broadcasting will evolve in the years ahead will turn largely on the way in which political society develops. If there are no certainties, and there are not, there are at least some probabilities. Foremost amongst these is that changes, when they come, will be gradual. They will creep up on us, if not exactly unobserved, at any rate in such a hesitant way that much of their deeper significance will be noted and pondered only by a few. Like the children's game, grandmother's footsteps, the end result becomes known only when it has arrived. Policies are likely to be piecemeal, following no grand design, their origins lying deep in the impacted soil of informed public opinion and its ubiquitous flower, consensus. Agreement on what generally seems to be regarded as the sensible thing to do is still the most powerful political influence in British life. However distasteful to radicals with a bolder and less patient view of what needs to be done, the evolutionary approach has had indisputable merits in the past.

Over the centuries, for example, it has enabled Britain to adapt to a totally changed industrialized world and a new social order in a peaceful and, on the whole, dignified way. Internal revolution and violent upheaval have been avoided, perhaps the most remarkable achievement of all in our modern political history. But this stability, for so long envied abroad as much or more than it has been prized at home, based on continuity, compromise and order, is unlikely to serve Britain as well in the future as in the past. Loss of Empire and below-average economic growth have contributed to an inward-looking national character not yet offset by any real feeling of identity with the other countries of Europe in membership of the European Communities. There are fewer wars or great issues to raise people's sights to broader horizons. Religion is in decline, while too often envy and resentment, also consequences of a weak economy with little prospect of growth, are apparent.

Greater leisure has resulted from a progressively shorter working week and longer holidays. The work ethic, while still alive, is no longer the dynamo it once was. Meanwhile a giant new power in the State has arrived in the form of the unions. Yet outside the negotiation of improved wages and conditions of work, the Trade Union movement has shown itself better at stopping things than at starting them. It is not alone in this: governments, political parties, the Civil Service and other pillars of the State are also frequently too negative, reacting to events rather than seeking to influence them in positive ways. The sheer burden of administration, the overloading of machines designed for another purpose or another age, has something to do with it. New governments coming fresh to the task, as was seen in 1979, can bring a briskness and determination that is much needed but is, nonetheless, hard to maintain over an extended period.

These observations amount to no more than a personal view of the background against which institutional change will take place over the next two decades until the end of the century. The picture is not so much one of inertia, but of habits outliving functions. In the broadcasting field one habit or convention, however, needs to be preserved above all else. This is the independence of the broadcaster from direct political control. Freedom of the air has been maintained by the broadcasting authorities acting as a buffer between the politicians and the programme makers. In the future the likelihood is that their role will be weakened since the broadcasting authorities will no longer control all the sources of programme material. Some may originate from outside the country, while others may be essentially local in origin and appeal, such as community radio or material produced for distribution on local cable systems. At the same time a vast flood of visual material recorded on tape or videodisc will be finding its way into people's homes. With the exception of an occasional documentary film, not much of this, in Britain at least, may be directly political in content. Some dramatic and entertainment material, however, will inevitably contain scenes of violence, sexual behaviour and even pornography, which are strictly regulated at present by the broadcasting authorities.

On a wider canvas there is a more political perspective. Audio cassettes, for instance, have already contributed to coups or revolutions overseas. In Iran it was reported that while the Shah tightly controlled the press and broadcasting, thousands of cassettes were circulating in the bazaars carrying the voice of the exiled Ayatollah.[16] Video recorders are popular in South Africa and the circulation of video cassettes is widespread. Neither the cassette listened to or viewed in private, nor the satellite broadcast beamed from space, can easily be restricted by the State. So the new communications technology points towards at least the possibility of a move away from the centralized control of the institutions of broadcasting which applies over so much of the world today. As Anthony Sampson commented in reviewing the international implications of some of these developments: 'This should be good news to anyone who believes in freedom of speech and opinions, and in the ultimate appeal of democratic values.[17]

In Britain, too, the institutions of broadcasting are likely to be radically effected, although here the news may not be altogether so good. It is difficult to forecast the future, but at some time during the next decade I expect programmes to begin to be received by way of satellite transmissions aimed direct to the home. Some broadcasts may originate from internationally authorized sources; others from private enterprise ventures like the radio pirates before them. Audiences might be small at first since special reception equipment would be required. The initial programming might consist of specialized material with a sharply focused audience appeal: sport and pop music almost certainly; something not far off pornography very probably. All of this would presumably be entirely free of any form of institutional control and would be conducted on a fairly low key. The profit at this stage might be small, but for the promoters there would be possibilities of using their material on videodisc and other spin-offs, as well as publicizing new and unknown stations. However imperceptible it might seem at the time, the first inexorable step would have been taken.

The second stage might see the building up of satellite broadcasts, perhaps not so slowly, to cover popular mass appeal programmes such as feature films, soap opera, quiz games, crime series and other US imports. Sex and violence might be portrayed to a higher extent than is now permitted, limited only by what was held by advertisers to be acceptable to family audiences. At this stage satellite broadcasting, unregulated and wholly market-oriented as it would be, could anticipate attracting strong support from advertisers and achieving high profits within a period of three to five years. The effect on the ecology of broadcasting cannot be predicted with any certainty, but it could be volcanic. There would be a great and growing loss of audience both by the BBC and Independent Television. In its turn this would lead to a great and growing loss of revenue by ITV. Within half a dozen years or so ITV might find itself strained to provide the resources to maintain a comprehensive service, whether on one channel or two. The BBC, if still financed from licence revenue, might be less affected, although the flight of much of its audience could only have the effect of undermining its already precarious financial position still further.

How would government and Parliament react in these circumstances? It must be doubtful whether the process could be stopped by regulation, any more than Radio Luxembourg or other broadcasters presently operating outside British territorial jurisdiction could be stopped. The necessary measures would probably be impracticable and too unpopular. Would it be feasible to join the gang in the way that Radio 1 did when the BBC was threatened by pirate radio? Possibly, but that would signal the end of ITV as it is now. The Independent Broadcasting Authority would be reduced to a residual role more similar to that of the American Federal Communications Commission, while the ITV companies would watch much of their revenue ebbing away. It may be that public policy would favour fighting it out, seeking to preserve the not inconsiderable audience that would still prefer the more mixed and solid fare offered by the BBC and ITV. If that were to be the case, it is hard to see that the bulk of advertising money would remain loyal to a regulated ITV in preference to unregulated broadcasts on a multiplicity of channels from satellites. The government of the day might find it worthwhile to maintain a public service system of broadcasting, at reduced cost, to satisfy the more discriminating audience and in order to maintain a national voice. Such a service would be far more vulnerable than the BBC has ever been in its history to political interference, and would divide the social classes to a disturbing degree.

Is all this too highly coloured, too alarmist a prospect?

Maybe it is, but at least it must be worth raising. For if events were to develop in this way institutional broadcasting as we now know it would be dealt a mortal blow. Finance would only be available for part of the current effort, while the career prospects of many who work in broadcasting would be destroyed. There would probably be room only for one public broadcasting service, and then in a very different form from what we know today.

Therefore a view of the future based on the rise of the media consumer and the fragmentation of the mass audience does not promise unqualified benefits. It is true that diversity and plurality in the supply of a wider range of programming, for viewing at times more convenient to the individual, are ends that are desirable in themselves. But even if the more dramatic of the developments outlined above do not in the event come to fruition, there are certainly going to be powerful challenges to traditional standards, as well as unprecedented opportunities to alter the map of broadcasting over the next two decades. The changes can be expected to be gradual at first, but as we approach the end of the century the pace will accelerate, threatening the independent sector, depending as it does on volatile advertising revenue, and the BBC alike. The British character, however, is skilled at adapting to new situations and it is to be hoped that there would be sufficient resolution and sufficient technical ingenuity to ensure that the fundamental principles which have grown up over the last fifty years are preserved, albeit in a different form.

For some time yet the existing broadcasting authorities, the BBC and the IBA, motivated as they have been since their inception by the concept of public service, will remain as prominent features on the institutional landscape of Britain. But their future is uncertain and there are no grounds whatever for complacency. On the contrary, the final chapter in the institutional history of broadcasting has begun. Who can say when or how it will end?

Appendix I

DECLARATION ON FUNDAMENTAL PRINCIPLES CONCERNING THE CONTRIBUTION OF THE MASS MEDIA TO STRENGTHENING PEACE AND INTERNATIONAL UNDERSTANDING, TO THE PROMOTION OF HUMAN RIGHTS AND TO COUNTERING RACIALISM, APARTHEID AND INCITEMENT TO WAR

Preamble

The General Conference,

Recalling that by virtue of its Constitution the purpose of Unesco is to 'contribute to peace and security by promoting collaboration among the nations through education, science and culture in order to further universal respect for justice, for the rule of law and for the human rights and fundamental freedoms' (Art. I, 1), and that to realize this purpose the Organization will strive 'to promote the free flow of ideas by word and image' (Art. I, 2),

Further recalling that under the Constitution the Member States of Unesco, 'believing in full and equal opportunities for education for all, in the unrestricted pursuit of objective truth, and in the free exchange of ideas and knowledge, are agreed and determined to develop and to increase the means of communication between their peoples and to employ these means for the purposes of mutual understanding and a truer and more perfect knowledge of each other's lives' (sixth preambular paragraph),

Recalling the purposes and principles of the United Nations, as specified in its Charter,

Recalling the Universal Declaration of Human Rights, adopted by the General Assembly of the United Nations in 1948 and particularly Article 19 thereof, which provides that 'everyone has the right to freedom of opinion and expression; this right includes freedom to hold opinions without interference and to seek, receive and impart information and ideas through any media and regardless of frontiers'; and the International Covenant on Civil and Political Rights, adopted by the General Assembly of the United Nations in 1966, Article 19 of which proclaims the same principles and Article 20 of which condemns incitement to war, the advocacy of national, racial or religious hatred and any form of discrimination, hostility or violence.

Recalling Article 4 of the International Convention on the Elimination of all Forms of Racial Discrimination, adopted by the General Assembly of the United Nations in 1965, and the International Convention on the Suppression and Punishment of the Crime of Apartheid, adopted by the General Assembly of the United Nations in 1973, whereby the States acceding to these Conventions undertook to adopt immediate and positive measures designed to eradicate all incitement to, or acts of, racial discrimination, and agreed to prevent any encouragement of the crime of apartheid and similar segregationist policies or their manifestations,

Recalling the Declaration on the Promotion among Youth of the Ideals of Peace, Mutual Respect and Understanding between Peoples, adopted by the General Assembly of the United Nations in 1965,

Recalling the declarations and resolutions adopted by the various organs of the United Nations concerning the establishment of a new international economic order and the role Unesco is called upon to play in this respect,

Recalling the Declaration of the Principles of International Cultural Co-operation, adopted by the General Conference of Unesco in 1966,

Recalling Resolution 59(I) of the General Assembly of the United Nations, adopted in 1946 and declaring:
'Freedom of information is a fundamental human right and is the touchstone of all the freedoms to which the United Nations is consecrated;

. . . .

Freedom of information requires as an indispensable element the willingness and capacity to employ its privileges without abuse. It requires as a basic discipline the moral obligation to seek the facts without prejudice and to spread knowledge without malicious intent;

....',

Recalling Resolution 110(II) of the General Assembly of the United Nations, adopted in 1947, condemning all forms of propaganda which are designed or likely to provoke or encourage any threat to the peace, breach of the peace, or act of aggression,

Recalling resolution 127(II), also adopted by the General Assembly in 1947, which invites Member States to take measures, within the limits of constitutional procedures, to combat the diffusion of false or distorted reports likely to injure friendly relations between States, as well as the other resolutions of the General Assembly concerning the mass media and their contribution to strengthening peace, trust and friendly relations among States,

Recalling resolution 9.12 adopted by the General Conference of Unesco in 1968, reiterating Unesco's objective to help to eradicate colonialism and racialism, and resolution 12.1 adopted by the General Conference in 1976, which proclaims that colonialism, neo-colonialism and racialism in all its forms and manifestations are incompatible with the fundamental aims of Unesco,

Recalling resolution 4.301 adopted in 1970 by the General Conference of Unesco on the contribution of the information media to furthering international understanding and co-operation in the interests of peace and human welfare, and to countering propaganda on behalf of war, racialism, apartheid and hatred among nations, and *aware* of the fundamental contribution that mass media can make to the realizations of these objectives,

Recalling the Declaration on Race and Racial Prejudice adopted by the General Conference of Unesco at its twentieth session,

Conscious of the complexity of the problems of information in modern society, of the diversity of solutions which have been offered to them, as evidenced in particular by the consideration given to them within Unesco, and of the legitimate

desire of all parties concerned that their aspirations, points of view and cultural identity be taken into due consideration,
Conscious of the aspirations of the developing countries for the establishment of a new, more just and more effective world information and communication order,
Proclaims on this twenty-eighth day of November 1978 this Declaration on Fundamental Principles concerning the Contribution of the Mass Media to Strengthening Peace and International Understanding, to the Promotion of Human Rights and to Countering Racialism, Apartheid and Incitement to War.

Article I

The strengthening of peace and international understanding, the promotion of human rights and the countering of racialism, apartheid and incitement to war demand a free flow and a wider and better balanced dissemination of information. To this end, the mass media have a leading contribution to make. This contribution will be the more effective to the extent that the information reflects the different aspects of the subject dealt with.

Article II

1. The exercise of freedom of opinion, expression and information, recognized as an integral part of human rights and fundamental freedoms, is a vital factor in the strengthening of peace and international understanding.
2. Access by the public to information should be guaranteed by the diversity of the sources and means of information available to it, thus enabling each individual to check the accuracy of facts and to appraise events objectively. To this end, journalists must have freedom to report and the fullest possible facilities of access to information. Similarly, it is important that the mass media be responsive to concerns of peoples and individuals, thus promoting the participation of the public in the elaboration of information.
3. With a view to the strengthening of peace and international understanding, to promoting human rights and to countering racialism, apartheid and incitement to war, the mass

media throughout the world, by reason of their role, contribute to promoting human rights, in particular by giving expression to oppressed peoples who struggle against colonialism, neo-colonialism, foreign occupation and all forms of racial discrimination and oppression and who are unable to make their voices heard within their own territories.

4. If the mass media are to be in a position to promote the principles of this Declaration in their activities, it is essential that journalists and other agents of the mass media, in their own country or abroad, be assured of protection guaranteeing them the best conditions for the exercise of their profession.

Article III

1. The mass media have an important contribution to make to the strengthening of peace and international understanding and in countering racialism, apartheid and incitement to war.
2. In countering aggressive war, racialism, apartheid and other violations of human rights which are *inter alia* spawned by prejudice and ignorance, the mass media, by disseminating information on the aims, aspirations, cultures and needs of all peoples, contribute to eliminate ignorance and misunderstanding between peoples, to make nationals of a country sensitive to the needs and desires of others, to ensure the respect of the rights and dignity of all nations, all peoples and all individuals without distinction of race, sex, language, religion or nationality and to draw attention to the great evils which afflict humanity, such as poverty, malnutrition and diseases, thereby promoting the formulation by States of the policies best able to promote the reduction of international tension and the peaceful and equitable settlement of international disputes.

Article IV

The mass media have an essential part to play in the eduction of young people in a spirit of peace, justice, freedom, mutual respect and understanding, in order to promote human rights, equality of rights as between all human beings and all nations, and economic and social progress. Equally, they have an important role to play in making known the views and aspirations of the younger generation.

Article V

In order to respect freedom of opinion, expression and information and in order that information may reflect all points of view, it is important that the points of view presented by those who consider that the information published or disseminated about them has seriously prejudiced their effort to strengthen peace and international understanding, to promote human rights or to counter racialism, apartheid and incitement to war be disseminated.

Article VI

For the establishment of a new equilibrium and greater reciprocity in the flow of information, which will be conducive to the institution of a just and lasting peace and to the economic and political independence of the developing countries, it is necessary to correct the inequalities in the flow of information to and from developing countries, and between those countries. To this end, it is essential that their mass media should have conditions and resources enabling them to gain strength and expand, and to co-operate both among themselves and with the mass media in developed countries.

Article VII

By disseminating more widely all of the information concerning the universally accepted objectives and principles which are the bases of the resolutions adopted by the different organs of the United Nations, the mass media contribute effectively to the strengthening of peace and international understanding, to the promotion of human rights, and to the establishment of a more just and equitable international economic order.

Article VIII

Professional organizations, and people who participate in the professional training of journalists and other agents of the mass media and who assist them in performing their functions in a responsible manner should attach special importance to the principles of this Declaration when drawing up and ensuring application of their codes of ethics.

Article IX

In the spirit of this Declaration, it is for the international community to contribute to the creation of the conditions for a free flow and wider and more balanced dissemination of information, and of the conditions for the protection, in the exercise of their functions, of journalists and other agents of the mass media. Unesco is well placed to make a valuable contribution in this respect.

Article X

1. With due respect for constitutional provisions designed to guarantee freedom of information and for the applicable international instruments and agreements, it is indispensable to create and maintain throughout the world the conditions which make it possible for the organizations and persons professionally involved in the dissemination of information to achieve the objectives of this Declaration.
2. It is important that a free flow and wider and better balanced dissemination of information be encouraged.
3. To this end, it is necessary that States facilitate the procurement by the mass media in the developing countries of adequate conditions and resources enabling them to gain strength and expand, and that they support co-operation by the latter both among themselves and with the mass media in developed countries.
4. Similarly, on a basis of equality of rights, mutual advantage and respect for the diversity of the cultures which go to make up the common heritage of mankind, it is essential that bilateral and multilateral exchanges of information among all States, and in particular between those which have different economic and social systems, be encouraged and developed.

Article XI

For this declaration to be fully effective it is necessary, with due respect for the legislative and administrative provisions and the other obligations of Member States, to guarantee the existence of favourable conditions for the operation of the mass media, in conformity with the provisions of the Universal Declaration of Human Rights and with the corresponding principles proclaimed in the International Covenant on Civil and Political Rights adopted by the General Assembly of the United Nations in 1966.

Appendix II

INTRODUCTION

1. All concerned in the making of programmes for Independent Television have to act within a series of constraints. They must take into account the degree of public concern about particular issues, the boundaries of public taste, the limits of the law and any available information from research about the short or longer-term social consequences of their actions. How should constraints like these affect their judgement about the presentation of scenes of violence on television?

2. The question arises why should violence have to be portrayed *at all* on television. The answers are clear. First, conflict is of the essence of drama, and conflict often leads to violence. Second, the real world contains much violence in many forms, and when television seeks to reflect the world – in fact or in fiction – it would be unrealistic and untrue to ignore its violent aspects.

3. Violence is not only physical: it can be verbal, psychological and even metaphysical or supernatural. Whatever form the violence in a programme may take its inclusion can only be justified by the dramatic or informational context in which it is seen, and the skill, insight and sensitivity of the portrayal.

4. Ideally, a Code should give a clear guide to behaviour based on reliable knowledge of the consequences of different decisions. Unfortunately, no Code of this kind can be provided. There are few relevant facts and few reliable findings derived from generally accepted research studies.

5. Nevertheless, it must be recognised that this is an area of public concern which extends to factual as well as fictional

programmes. People fear that violence on the television screen
may be harmful, either to the individual viewer (particularly if
the viewer is a child) or to society as a whole.
6. This public concern arises for various reasons, and may
refer to different kinds of assumed 'effect';
i At the simplest level, some portrayed acts of violence may
   go *beyond the bounds of what is tolerable* for the average
   viewer. These could be classified as material which, in the
   words of the Television Act, 'offend against good taste or
   decency' or 'is likely to be offensive to public feeling'.
ii There is portrayed violence which is potentially so disturbing
   that it might be *psychologically harmful*, particularly for
   young or emotionally insecure viewers.
iii Violence portrayed on television *may be imitated* in a real-
   life situation.
iv The regular and recurrent spectacle of violence might lead
   viewers to think violence in one form or another has been
   given the stamp of approval. Once violence is thus accepted
   and tolerated people will, it is believed, tend to become *more
   callous*, more indifferent to the suffering imposed on the
   victims of violence.
7. Public concern is reflected in the Television Act of 1964,
which requires the Independent Television Authority to draw
up a Code giving guidance about the showing of violence,
particularly 'when large numbers of children and young persons
may be expected to be watching'. The Act also requires the
Authority to ensure that nothing is included in the programmes
which '. . . is likely to encourage or incite to crime or to lead to
disorder or to be offensive to public feeling'.
8. The accompanying new Code replaces the one that has been
in use since 1964. It has been prepared by a Working Party on
the Portrayal of Violence in Programmes which was set up in
October 1970 and which has taken into account the state of
present knowledge and the results of available research. It is
intended that this Code should be kept under constant review
and revised as and when necessary in the light of new developments and the results of continuing research studies.
9. The responsibility for particular care when many children
and young persons may be viewing is the reason for the adoption
of the 'family viewing policy' in Independent Television. The

portrayal of violence is one of the main considerations which determine whether or not a programme is suitable for transmission during 'family viewing time'. Programmes shown before 9.00 p.m. should not be unsuitable for an audience in which children are present.

THE CODE

All concerned in the planning, production and scheduling of television programmes must keep in mind the following considerations:

The Content of the Programme Schedule as a Whole

(a) People seldom view just one programme. An acceptable minimum of violence in each individual programme may add up to an intolerable level over a period.

(b) The time of screening of each programme is important. Adults may be expected to tolerate more than children can. The ITV policy of 'family viewing time' until 9.00 p.m. entails special concern for younger viewers.

The Ends and the Means

(c) There is no evidence that the portrayal of violence for good or 'legitimate' ends is likely to be less harmful to the individual, or to society, than the portrayal of violence for evil ends.

Presentation

(d) There is no evidence that 'sanitised' or 'conventional' violence, in which the consequences are concealed, minimised or presented in a ritualistic way, is innocuous. It may be just as dangerous to society to conceal the results of violence or to minimise them as to let people see clearly the full consequences of violent behaviour, however gruesome: what may be better for society may be emotionally more upsetting or more offensive for the individual viewer.

(e) Violence which is shown as happening long ago or far away may seem to have less impact on the viewer, but it remains violence. Horror in costume remains horror.

(f) Dramatic truth may occasionally demand the portrayal of a sadistic character, but there can be no defence of violence shown solely for its own sake, or of the gratuitous exploitation of sadistic or other perverted practices.

(g) Ingenious and unfamiliar methods of inflicting pain or injury – particularly if capable of easy imitation – should not be shown without the most careful consideration.

(h) Violence has always been and still is widespread throughout the world, so violent scenes in news and current affairs programmes are inevitable. But the editor or producer must be sure that the *degree* of violence shown is essential to the integrity and completeness of his programme.

The Young and the Vulnerable

(i) Scenes which may unsettle young children need special care. Insecurity is less tolerable for a child – particularly an emotionally unstable child – than for a mature adult. Violence, menace and threats can take many forms – emotional, physical and verbal. Scenes of domestic friction, whether or not accompanied by physical violence, can easily cause fear and insecurity.

(j) Research evidence shows that the socially or emotionally insecure individual, particularly if adolescent, is specially vulnerable. There is also evidence that such people tend to be more dependent on television than are others. Imagination, creativity or realism on television cannot be constrained to such an extent that the legitimate service of the majority is always subordinated to the limitations of a minority. But a civilised society pays special attention to its weaker members.

This Code cannot provide universal rules. The programme maker must carry responsibility for his own decisions. In so sensitive an area risks require special justification. If in doubt, cut.

Notes

Chapter 1: The Case for Press Freedom

1. *A History of the English-Speaking Peoples*, Vol. I: *The Birth of Britain* (Cassell, London, 1956) p. xvii.

2. See Williams, Francis, *Nothing so Strange* (Cassell, London, 1970) pp. 168–9. Mr Williams, a former Fleet Street editor, was Controller of News and Censorship at the Ministry of Information at the time.

3. Much has been written about this episode, and the extent of the action threatened by the Prime Minister is still not clearly established. The definitive account is contained in Briggs, Asa, *Governing the BBC* (British Broadcasting Corporation, London, 1979) pp. 209–17.

4. For a full discussion of the nature of political communication see Windlesham, Lord, *Communication and Political Power* (Jonathan Cape, London, 1965) Chapter 1.

5. Siebert, F. S., Peterson, T. and Schramm, W., *Four Theories of the Press* (University of Illinois Press, Urbana, 1963) p. 2; and Siebert, F. S., *Freedom of the Press In England 1476–1776* ((University of Illinois Press, Urbana, 1952).

6. The wording of the title of the draft declaration was amended in the course of the conference by substituting the words 'contribution . . . to' for 'use . . . in'.

7. *The Times* 17 November 1978.

8. Righter, Rosemary, *Whose News? Politics, the Press and the Third World* (Burnett Books, London, 1978) p. 23.

9. Righter, *Whose News?*, p. 134. In a chapter headed 'UNESCO—Medium for the New Message', Mrs Righter traces in intricate detail the history of UNESCO's involvement in the controversy over international communications policy; see pp. 134–81.

10. Letter from the International Press Institute's Director, *The Times* 2 November 1978.

11. *The Times* 17 November 1978.

12. *The Observer* 22 October 1978.

13. Dr Tom Margerison, as reported in *The Times* 23 November 1978.

14. *The Observer* 26 November 1978.

15. On 8 December 1979 the *Guardian* published an article titled 'Only Connect' by Mervyn Jones which gave a very full and informative account

of the work of the UNESCO International Commission for the Study of Communication Problems.

16. *The Economist* 25 November 1978, p. 72.
17. *The Granada Guildhall Lecture 1975* (Hart-Davis, MacGibbon, London, 1975).
18. *The Times* 17 December 1979.

CHAPTER 2: The Rise of Broadcasting

1. The BBC was not in fact the first public corporation as is sometimes suggested. Earlier examples include the Port of London Authority (1908) and the Forestry Commission (1919). But it was the most conspicuous.
2. Clayre, Alasdair, *The Impact of Broadcasting* or *Mrs Buckle's Wall is Singing* (Compton Russell (by arrangement with the BBC) London, 1973) p. 11.
3. Briggs, Asa, *The History of Broadcasting in the United Kindgom* (Oxford University Press, London) Vol. I, *The Birth of Broadcasting*, was published in 1961, followed by Vol. II, *The Golden Age of Wireless*, in 1965. Vol. III, *The War of Words* (1970), covered the war-time period between 1939–45, while Vol. IV, *Sound and Vision* (1979), takes the history of the British broadcasting up to the start of Independent Television in 1955.
4. Later Sir John Reith (1927) and Lord Reith (1940). Reith left the BBC in 1938 in order to become Chairman of Imperial Airways and never returned to broadcasting. A strong opponent of commercial television, he improbably and unsuccessfully applied for a post at the Independent Television Authority in 1954. See Clark, Kenneth, *The Other Half* (John Murray, London, 1977) pp. 138–9.
5. Reith, J. C. W., *Broadcast over Britain* (Hodder & Stoughton, London, 1924) p. 17.
6. Clayre, *The Impact of Broadcasting*, p. 12.
7. The colour licence fee was raised to £34 in November 1979.
8. *Report of the Broadcasting Committee, 1925* (Cmnd. 2599, HMSO, London, 1926).
9. This abstract is quoted from Paulu, Burton, *British Broadcasting* (University of Minnesota Press, Minneapolis, 1956) pp. 32–3.
10. Briggs, *The History of Broadcasting*, Vol. I, p. 363.
11. ibid., p. 362.
12. ibid., pp. 361–2.
13. James, Robert Rhodes, *Churchill: a Study in Failure 1900–1939* (Weidenfeld and Nicolson, London, 1970) p. 174.
14. Quoted in *BBC Handbook 1957* (British Broadcasting Corporation, London) p. 13 and also, with approval, by the Pilkington Committee:

Report of the Committee on Broadcasting, 1960 (Cmnd. 1753, HMSO, London, 1962) p. 116.

15. Hansard *HC Debates* 10 December 1929 col. 246.

16. *Broadcasting Committee: Report* (Cmnd. 1951, HMSO, London, 1923).

17. *Report of the Broadcasting Committee, 1935* (Cmnd. 5091, HMSO, London, 1936).

18. See Briggs, Asa, *Governing the BBC* (British Broadcasting Corporation, London, 1979) p. 276.

19. Briggs, *The History of Broadcasting*, Vol. II, p. 421. See also *Observations* by the Board of Governors of the BBC on the Report of the Broadcasting Committee, 1935, p. 2.

20. Formerly John Harris, an ex-journalist who had been Director of Publicity for the Labour Party in 1962–4 and later a member of the editorial staff of the *Economist*. Harris had previously been special assistant to Roy Jenkins, both as Chancellor of the Exchequer (1967–70) and during an earlier period as Home Secretary in 1965–7. He was created a life peer and Minister of State, Home Office, in 1974.

21. Sir Robert Armstrong became Permanent Under Secretary of State at the Home Office in 1977. He had been Principal Private Secretary both to Mr Heath and Sir Harold Wilson at No. 10 Downing Street, 1970–5. He was appointed as Secretary of the Cabinet in 1979. Philip Woodfield, a Deputy Secretary at the Home Office since 1974, has had general oversight of broadcasting policy.

22. *Television: The Journal of the Royal Television Society* (March/April 1979) p. 5.

23. Originally known as the Independent Television Authority when set up by Act of Parliament in 1954. The name was changed to the Independent Broadcasting Authority when responsibility for local sound broadcasting services was added in 1972.

24. This chapter was written before the publication of Briggs, *Governing the BBC* in November 1979. The author was relieved to find that it coincides generally with Asa Briggs' study of who were the BBC governors between 1927–78; their powers and performance; and their relationships with the director-general, BBC management and government. The book also contains nine detailed case studies of controversial incidents in which the governors have been involved and is required reading for anyone who wishes to pursue this subject at greater length.

25. Lord Reith later gave his side of this troubled relationship in his memoirs. See *Into the World* (Hodder & Stoughton, London, 1949) pp. 114–27. Clarendon was shown this account before publication and responded generously.

26. Mary Agnes Hamilton, quoted in Briggs, *The History of Broadcasting*, Vol. II, p. 433.

27. ibid., p. 431.

28. *BBC Lunch-time Lectures Fourth Series—3* 15 December 1965 (British Broadcasting Corporation, London, No. 3/6431).

29. Hill, *Behind the Screen: The Broadcasting Memoirs of Lord Hill* (Sidgwick and Jackson, London, 1974) p. 17.

30. *The Third Floor Front: a View of Broadcasting in the Sixties* (The Bodley Head, London, 1969) pp. 13–14.

31. Hill, *Behind the Screen*, pp. 72–81.

32. ibid., p. 78. The remark is attributed to David Attenborough.

33. ibid., pp. 70–1.

34. This incident is described in Briggs, *Governing the BBC*, pp. 227–31. Lord Hill has also provided his own account in *Behind the Screen*, pp. 217–28.

35. Hill, *Behind the Screen*, p. 262. It is fair to say that Lord Hill's version has been challenged by Sir Hugh Greene in a hostile review of *Behind the Screen* in the *New Statesman* (20 September 1974). Asa Briggs is also sceptical regarding some of Hill's claims, see *Governing the BBC*, pp. 34–45.

36. Briggs, *Governing the BBC*, p. 45.

CHAPTER 3: Competition: Then and Now

1. Goodhardt, G. J., Ehrenberg, A. S. C., and Collins, M. A., *The Television Audience: Patterns of Viewing* (Saxon House & Lexington Books, London & New York, 1975) p. ix.

2. JICTAR Establishment Surveys 1970–77; JICTAR Forecast Establishment Surveys 1978–79.

3. Briggs, *The History of Broadcasting*, Vol. IV, contains a table showing the numbers of sound and television licences between 1947–55 at p. 240.

4. *Television Act, 1954*, 2 & 3 Eliz. II, Ch. 55, Second Schedule: Rules as to Advertisements (1) p. 20.

5. *Report of the Broadcasting Committee, 1949* (Cmnd. 8116, HMSO, London, 1951).

6. Butler, R. A., *The Art of the Possible: the Memoirs of Lord Butler* (Hamish Hamilton, London, 1971) p. 172.

7. Christopher Mayhew, MP, had been primarily concerned in establishing the National Television Council in 1953. Its aims were 'to resist the introduction of commercial television into this country and to encourage the healthy development of public service television in the national interest'. See Briggs, *The History of Broadcasting*, Vol. IV, p. 896.

8. *The Economist* 15 August 1953. Quoted in Briggs, *The History of Broadcasting*, Vol. IV, p. 909.

9. Briggs, *The History of Broadcasting* reprints verbatim a Labour Party leaflet attacking commercial television titled 'Not fit for children?' (Vol. IV, p. 897).

10. *New Statesman* 21 July 1961, p. 85.

11. *Books and Bookmen*, Vol. 24 (1979) p. 12.

12. Briggs, *The History of Broadcasting*, Vol. IV, pp. 896–7.

13. *Pressure Group: The Campaign for Commercial Television* (Secker and Warburg, London, 1961).

14. *The Listener* 15 March 1979, p. 372.

15. *Independent Broadcasting* No. 19 (1979) p. 13.

16. *Report of an ITA Consultation on Regional Programmes* held at Newcastle upon Tyne (November 1968) p. 2.

17. ibid., p. 2.

18. *Report of the Committee on the Future of Broadcasting* (Cmnd. 6753, HMSO, London, 1977) pp. 150–3.

19. ibid., p. 153.

20. ibid., p. 73.

21. *Broadcasting* (Cmnd. 7294, HMSO, London, 1978) p. 21.

22. *Report of the Committee on the Future of Broadcasting*, p. 90.

23. ibid., p. 72.

24. *Broadcasting*, pp. 45–6.

CHAPTER 4: Television: The Programme Makers

1. Hansard *House of Commons Debates* 15 May 1979 col. 51.

2. Transcript of speech made by the Home Secretary (issued by the Home Office 14 September 1978) p. 8.

3. *The Fourth Channel: the Authority's Proposals* (published statement by the IBA 12 November 1979) p. 6.

4. See *The Economist* 12 January 1980, *Financial Times* 11 January 1980, and *The Times* 14 January 1980.

5. Forman, Denis, 'TV: some mysteries of the organism', *The Royal Television Society Journal* (July/August 1973) p. 233.

6. Burns, Tom, *The BBC: Public Institution and Private World* (Macmillan, London, 1977).

7. *Broadcast* magazine 23 April 1979, p. 15.

8. Forman, 'TV: some mysteries of the organism'.

9. Burns, *The BBC*, pp. 122–3.

10. Random House, New York, 1967.

11. See Glasgow University Media Study Group, *Bad News* (Routledge & Kegan Paul, London, 1976). An interesting study on the way the BBC reports the news is Schlesinger, Philip, *Putting 'Reality' Together* (Constable, London, 1978).

12. IBA Lecture on 'Freedom and Censorship' published in *Independent Broadcasting* No. 20 (1979) pp. 17–24.
13. *Second Progress Report and Recommendations* (Leicester University Press, 1969).
14. ibid., p. 34.
15. BBC Publications, London, 1972.
16. Saxon House, London, 1978.
17. Maurice Temple Smith, London, 1978.
18. *Report of the Committee on the Future of Broadcasting* (Cmnd. 6753-I HMSO, London, 1977) Appendix F, pp. 29–73.
19. *The Portrayal of Violence on Television, BBC and IBA Guidelines* (BBC and IBA, London, 1980).
20. Faber, London, 1977.

CHAPTER 5: Radio finds a New Role

1. Oxford University Press, London, 1965.
2. ibid., p. 6.
3. (Sir) Ivone Kirkpatrick, Director of the Foreign Division of the Ministry of Information in 1940, was appointed as Controller of the BBC's European Services in 1941. He was later to become Permanent Under-Secretary of State at the Foreign Office (1953–7) and Chairman of the Independent Television Authority (1957–62).
4. *Report of the Broadcasting Committee, 1949* (Cmnd. 8116, HMSO, London, 1951) p. 5.
5. ibid., p. 9.
6. Now Lord Glenamara.
7. Hansard *HC Debates* 15 February 1967 col. 640.
8. Singer, Aubrey, speech titled 'Radio and the Eighties: Art and Utility' delivered on 23 August 1979 to a BBC/IBA Seminar at the Royal College of Physicians, Edinburgh.
9. Curran, Charles, *A Seamless Robe: Broadcasting—Philosophy and Practice* (Collins, London, 1979) p. 161.
10. Larkin, Philip, *High Windows* (Faber & Faber, London, 1974) p. 34.
11. Levin, Bernard, *The Pendulum Years* (Cape, London, 1970) p. 318.
12. Hansard *HC Debates* report of the second reading of The Marine Broadcasting Offences Bill, 1967 15 February 1967 cols. 630–1.
13. Paul Bryan's team was an impressive one. His deputy as Opposition Front Bench spokesman on Broadcasting was Ian Gilmour, while the background research was carried out by Christopher Patten, later director of the Conservative Research Department, and since 1979 MP for Bath.
14. Curran, *A Seamless Robe*, p. 162.
15. Hansard *HC Debates* 29 March 1971 col. 1166.

16. See *10th Report from Select Committee on Nationalised Industries (Session 1977–78) on the Independent Broadcasting Authority—Observations by the Home Secretary and the IBA* (Cmnd. 7791, HMSO, London, 1979).
17. John Thompson had been on the editorial staff of the *Daily Express* from 1957–9, was editor of *Time and Tide* 1960–2, and joined the *Observer* as News Editor in 1962. He was editor of the *Observer* Colour Magazine from 1966–70.
18. *Journal of the Royal Society of Arts*, Vol. CXXVI (1978) p. 564.
19. *Independent Local Radio: Looking to the Future* a report published by the IBA Radio Division in July 1979, pp. 3–4.
20. *Neighbourhood Radio in Wales*, a report published by the BBC, Cardiff, in January 1979.
21. *Report of the Committee on the Future of Broadcasting* (Cmnd. 6753, HMSO, London, 1977) p. 205.
22. ibid., p. 206.
23. *Broadcasting* (Cmnd. 7294, HMSO, London, 1978) p. 15.
24. See Singer, *Radio and the Eighties*, p. 27.

CHAPTER 6: Institutional Broadcasting

1. The allocated position for the UK satellite is 31°W, 500 miles off the coast of Brazil. Most other countries of Europe, including France, West Germany, Belgium, Luxembourg and Switzerland have been allocated satellite positions at 10°W. Spain shares the same position as the UK, while Denmark is at 5°E.
2. Transcript of a *Consultation on Engineering Research and Development in Independent Television* (Independent Broadcasting Authority, London, 1979) p. 22.
3. ibid., p. 22.
4. *Report of the Committee on the Future of Broadcasting* (Cmnd. 6753, HMSO, London, 1977) p. 3.
5. The reference to the same service does not seem to take account of the fact that the present limited television service in India, covering only 8% of the country by area and 15% by population, calls for programming in twelve languages (see *Television/Radio Age International* September 1979, p. A-56).
6. *Report of the Committee on the Future of Broadcasting*, p. 385.
7. Transcript of a speech to the Royal Television Society's Convention at King's College, Cambridge, 15 September 1979, pp. 1–2.
8. The annual cost of the United Kingdom's contributions to the European Space Agency has been as follows:

1974/75	£19.6 million
1975/76	£29.1 million

1976/77	£38.3 million
1977/78	£39.5 million
1978/79	£40.4 million

9. These statistics were contained in a special survey on Satellites published by the *Financial Times* 1 August 1979, p. 11.

10. British technology and manufacturing capacity in the aerospace, electronics, telecommunications, scientific and power systems fields have been utilized in other programmes of the European Space Agency. Since 1972 the total value of ESA contracts placed in Britain amounts to approximately £180.5 millions (as at December 1979).

11. Figures based on an article by P. Harker, Principal Engineering Information Officer, IBA, published in *Viewpoint* (ITCA, London) Autumn 1979, p. 4.

12. *The Times* 11 May 1965. An off-print of this article was included in the published report of the seminar, titled *The Future of Commercial Television 1965–1975*.

13. Harker, in *Viewpoint*, p. 4.

14. Toshiba in Japan is experimenting with a video tape player based on a relatively short length of magnetic tape, probably about 19", with a great many longitudinal tracks. The advantage of such a system is that it could be duplicated in a real time of seconds rather than hours, with a consequential reduction in the cost of pre-recorded cassettes.

15. Benn, A. *Arguments for Socialism* (Jonathan Cape, London, 1979) p. 178.

16. See Sampson, Anthony, 'Coups by cassette and cathode ray', *The Observer* 13 January 1980.

17. ibid.

INDEX

ABC Television, 82
Access to broadcasting, 14, 127–9, 132–3, 137–8, 146–8
Advertising Advisory Committee, 88, 89
Agence France Presse, 9
Alcohol advertising, 89
American Forces Network, 111
Anglia TV, 59
Annan Committee on the Future of Broadcasting, 28–9, 48, 57, 58, 59, 60, 62, 64, 65, 71, 72, 73, 76, 98, 117, 123, 124, 132, 133
Ariane, rocket launcher, 134
Armstrong, (Sir) Robert, 29
Associated Press, 9
Associated-Rediffusion, 82
Attlee, Clement (Earl Attlee), 52
ATV, 58, 60, 82
Audio cassettes, 146–7
Aylestone, Lord, 38

Bad language, 86, 90
Baldwin, Stanley (Earl Baldwin), 23
Baverstock, Donald, 84
BBC (British Broadcasting Corporation)
  audience, 21, 63, 148
  audience research department, 98
  Eden and, 1
  governors, 31–2, 36–9, 64, 67, 69–70, 79
  Hill as chairman, 33–6
  history, 18–42, 104
  IBA and, 39, 106–7
  licences, 20–1, 24
  Post Office and, 19–24, 26–8
  pressures on, 14–15
  professionalism v. public service, 80–5
  programmes, see Programme
  public opinion and, 25–6, 38
  radio, 41, 104–14, 119–26
  splitting up, 72
  State and, 21–4, 41–2, 104–5, 147–8
  TV, 60–6, 69, 75, 106–7
  violence and, 99
  Wilson and, 2, 36
BBC 1, 60, 61–3, 64, 66, 69, 75
BBC 2, 60, 61–3, 65
Beeching, Dr R. (Lord Beeching), 38
Belson, Dr W. A., 98
Benn, Tony, 144
Beveridge Committee on Broadcasting, 28, 37, 48, 49, 72, 105–6
BMA, 89
Briggs, Asa (Lord Briggs), 19, 38, 52, 103
Britain Radio, 111
British Gazette, 23–4
Bryan, (Sir) Paul, 113
Burgess, Sir John, 115
Burns, Professor Tom, 80, 83
Butler, R. A. (Lord Butler), 49, 52, 97

Cable systems, 133, 138, 139, 141, 143, 146
Cadogan, Sir Alexander, 46
Carter, Lady Violet Bonham, 47, 50
Ceefax, 139

Censorship, 93
Centre for Mass Communication Research, Leicester University, 97–8
Chapman-Walker, Mark, 52
Chataway, Christopher, 28–9, 114, 115
Churchill, (Sir) Winston, 1, 23–4, 52, 105
Cinema, 19, 94, 98
Clarendon, Lord, 31–2
Code of Advertising Standards and Practice, 88, 90
Collins, Norman, 46, 51, 52
Competition in broadcasting, 43–6, 63–70, 76
Coronation Street, 97
Cowell, Adrian, 60
Cowgill, Bryan, 68
Crawford Committee on Broadcasting, 22–3, 27
Croll, P., 98
Crossroads, 97
Cumbrian Newspapers, 115
Curran, Sir Charles, 37, 110, 114

Daily Mirror, 1, 48

Early Bird, 130
Economist, The, 50
Eden, Anthony Sir, (Earl of Avon), 1, 52
Eisenhower, Dr Milton, 96
Elizabeth R, 62
European Broadcasting Union, 7, 65, 135
European Space Agency, 134–7
Eysenck, Professor H. J. and Nias, D. K. N., 98

Fair Trading, Office of, 69
fforde, Sir Arthur, 34
Films, 10, 138, 146
Forman, Sir Denis, 77
Fraser, Sir Robert, 33–4, 55–6, 58, 114
Freedom, personal, 14
  broadcasting and, 2, 17–18, 21–2, 30, 41–2, 85–6, 93–4, 142, 146
  personal, 14
  press, 1–17
Freeman, John, 133
Frequency allocation, 108–9, 111–13, 127–8, 144–5
Friendly, Fred W., 83
Future of broadcasting, 130–9, 145–9

General Strike, 23
George V, King, 21
Gillard, Frank, 107–8
Goldie, Grace Wyndham, 80, 85
Granada TV, 58, 60, 64, 77, 82
Grandstand, 66
Greene, Sir Hugh, 34–5, 36, 37, 81
Growth of broadcasting, 40

Haley, Sir William, 46, 51
Halifax, Earl of, 50
Halloran, Professor, J., 98
Harris of Greenwich, Lord, 29
Hart, Dame Judith, 8
Heath, Edward, 28, 36